TECHNOLOGY UNBOUND:

*Transferring Scientific
and Engineering Resources
from Defense to Civilian Purposes*

TECHNOLOGY UNBOUND:

*Transferring Scientific
and Engineering Resources
from Defense to Civilian Purposes*

by

STEVEN R. RIVKIN

PERGAMON PRESS

NEW YORK • TORONTO • OXFORD • LONDON • MEXICO CITY
EDINBURGH • SYDNEY • PARIS • BRAUNSCHWEIG • TOKYO
BUENOS AIRES

PERGAMON PRESS INC.
Maxwell House, Fairview Park Elmsford, New York 10523

PERGAMON OF CANADA LTD.
207 Queen's Quay West, Toronto 1

PERGAMON PRESS LTD.
Headington Hill Hall, Oxford;
4 & 5 Fitzroy Square, London W. 1

PERGAMON PRESS S. A.
Villalongin 32, Mexico 5, D. F.

PERGAMON PRESS (SCOTLAND) LTD.
2 & 3 Teviot Place, Edinburgh 1

PERGAMON PRESS (AUST.) PTY. LTD.
Rushcutters Bay, Sydney, N.S.W.

PERGAMON PRESS S. A. R. L.
24 rue des Ecoles, Paris 5e

VIEWEG & SOHN GmbH
Burgplatz 1, Braunschweig

PERGAMON PRESS DIVISION
Barton Trading K. K.
French Bank Building
1-1-2 Akasaka, Minato-ku
Tokyo

Copyright (c) 1968, Pergamon Press Inc.
First Edition 1968
Library of Congress Catalog Card No. 68-59148

Printed in United States of America by McGregor & Werner, Inc.

08 006424 8 hard
08 006391 8 soft

For Marian

CONTENTS

FOREWORD

As AN OFFICIAL of an agency with responsibilities in the area covered by Mr. Rivkin's book, I welcome the kind of effort, independent of the government, which the book represents. It strikes the reader as a serious and objective analysis.

The book is an interesting contribution to a subject which has become even more important — because of increased defense expenditures due to Vietnam — since the book was written. The author considers, first, how serious the problem of transition for scientists and engineers will be from substantial (say the equivalent of 10 per cent of the gross national product) to reduced war production resulting from lower defense expenditures, and second, how this transition can best serve the United States by permitting us to meet some of the now unmet needs — for example, the renovation of cities and the restoration of fresh air and clean water.

The author refers to some of the work done by others in the field, up to 1966, and he reaches a reasoned and sanguine conclusion as to our country's ability to surmount the dislocations which might follow decreased defense expenditures. This same conclusion was stated by William C. Foster, Director of the U. S. Arms Control and Disarmament Agency, as follows:

> "It is now much more widely understood that the Federal Government can sustain demand either by reducing taxes and thus stimulating the private sector, or by increasing public expenditures, or by a judicious combination of the two."

Mr. Rivkin is also sanguine as to our ability to turn the resources released to more constructive purpose. Of course, the fact that we have the capability of doing this does not insure that we will have the desire or the will-power. We cannot have the desire and the willpower unless we are aware of the situation, and it is to be hoped that Mr. Rivkin's book will inform and persuade. At present, many American citizens remain unpersuaded of the desirability of greater, and necessarily more expensive, efforts to deal with our society's ills.

The first major opportunity for a decision is likely to present itself after the hostilities in Vietnam are over. That is why Mr. Rivkin's book is specially timely. It is also timely because, in the long run, the limiting of defense expenditures will improve the chance of meeting more of our other needs, and many arms control measures can contribute to limiting defense expenditures. This is particularly true of measures — like the limitation and reduction of offensive and defensive strategic nuclear weapons — which might follow the coming into effect of the Non-Proliferation Treaty recently signed by the United States, the Soviet Union, the United Kingdom, and over 75 other nations.

ARCHIBALD S. ALEXANDER
Assistant Director
U. S. Arms Control and
Disarmament Agency

September 11, 1968

PREFACE

THIS REPORT was written in the late summer of 1966. When the invitation to prepare it for publication was made a year later, little had occurred to alter its conclusions with regard to the problems and opportunities for converting American scientific and engineering resources from military to civilian purposes. The levels of current military expenditures set forth in the report have, however, been overtaken by the grueling circumstance of America's continuing involvement in the Vietnam war, levels of investment that will have to be scaled down at that time, earnestly desired, when the war diminishes its calls for men, machines, and energies of the American people. Meanwhile, and at least in part as a result of the drain of resources away from the urgent domestic problems outlined in this report, ghettoes in dozens of northern American cities exploded in frustration and violence in the summer of 1967, making even more urgent the tasks of domestic renewal outlined in this report. Now, in January 1968, the continuance of the war in Vietnam is the single most prominent barrier to the reallocation of effort and resources needed to meet these crucial domestic problems.

Yet, the demands of the war in Vietnam have not as yet changed the basic pattern of stability characteristic of American defense planning in the mid-1960's.

Even the decision to construct a thin Anti-Ballistic Missile defense announced in September 1967 is not expected to alter the character of defense spending significantly in the next half-decade, and consequently the nature of the long-term conversion problems facing the American economy. Most of the Vietnam-induced demands are in the ordnance and human support (e.g., food and uniforms) areas, where the past post-war experiences suggest that resources are readily convertible to allied civilian fields. Nonetheless, intensive post-Vietnam planning has begun within the U.S. Government in response to President Johnson's belief, announced in his 1967 Economic Report,* that:

> "When hostilities do end, we will be faced with a great opportunity and a challenge how best to use that opportunity. The resources now being claimed by the war can be diverted to peaceful uses both at home and abroad, and can hasten the attainment of the great goals upon which we have set our sights.

> "If we keep our eyes firmly fixed on these goals — and if we plan wisely — we need have no fear that the bridge from war to peace will exact a wasteful toll of idle resources, human or material."

But domestic events have not waited for the world to settle itself to fit the goals of U.S. foreign policy. The eruptions of Negro neighborhoods in Detroit and Newark have lent awesome additional weight to the needs of the Negro community for pervasive social and economic advancement. Nor are the problems of poverty confined solely to the non-white segment of the American population, as Gunnar Myrdal, the Swedish sociologist and student of American society, has

*Economic Report of the President, Washington, D.C. G.P.O., 1967; P. 23.

recently been careful to emphasize. And, for all the American people, there remain the vastly expensive needs for improved public facilities that are estimated by an authoritative study of the Congress' Joint Economic Committee to require a $500 billion investment in the next decade,* broadly confirming the projections of the National Planning Association study cited frequently in this report.

At the outset of the 1968 election year, the Vietnam war is very much on the minds of the American people. Hopefully, that problem will soon diminish its demands on American resources, though in a troubled world other overseas commitments may rise to take its place. Meanwhile, other, non-military problems facing the American people will never ease, unless and until major national efforts are directed toward their solution. Nor will the opportunities for the creative application of technology, which this report identifies as vital tools in attacking these needs, in any way grow less.

STEVEN R. RIVKIN

State and Local Public Facility Needs and Financing, study prepared for the Subcommittee on Economic Progress of the Joint Economic Committee, 89th Cong., 2nd Sess.; Washington G.P.O., 1966; Vol. 1, pp. 11-19.

INTRODUCTION

As THIS report is being written, the Gross National Product of the United States is running at an estimated rate of 732 billion dollars for the year 1966. One highly significant indicator of the strength of economic demand, the rate of unemployment, stands at less than 4 per cent of the labor force,[1] a figure unequalled in more than a dozen years.* There are at present no signs that the current growth of the American economy, which has now continued for an unprecedented 67 straight months, will soon abate. In fact, there is every

*Unquestionably, increased expenditures by the Federal Government to meet defense objectives in Vietnam — now budgeted at $10.3 billion in the current Fiscal Year (FY 1967) — account for a part of the continuing boom of the American economy. Prior to the beginning of special procurements for Vietnam in mid-1965, however, the expansionary effect of increasing business investments to serve the vigorous national market for goods and services was already apparent, and prosperity had continued uninterrupted *despite* a two-year drop in the proportion of defense purchases to Gross National Product, from 9.2 per cent in 1962 to 7.4 per cent in the first half of 1965. See *The Economic Report of the President and The Annual Report of the Council of Economic Advisers,* January 1966 (Washington, D.C., U.S.G.P.O.); especially pages 54 to 62. The war in Vietnam, in psychological terms as well as in its economic effects, constitutes an exception

(Continued next page)

reasonable expectation that within a decade the annual value of the Gross National Product of the United States will mount to one trillion dollars.

Yet few economists or planners in the United States can derive more than partial satisfaction from these statistical measures of prosperity. The nation is acutely aware of the scale and complexity of the manifold tasks that these resources must serve in the years ahead. With an increasing number and proportion of the American population crowding into metropolitan areas, whole cities must be rebuilt, and urgent solutions must be found to the problems of pollution in the environment and congested and inefficient urban and inter-urban transportation. Vast investments in goods and services will be required to provide new places for young people in educational institutions, to train new teachers, and to adapt both the content and methods of education at all levels to a world of increasing complexity and sophistication. The problems of the chronically poor and disadvantaged, in both urban and rural areas, plague the national conscience and demand prompt and com-

-----

to the general stability that has come to characterize the U.S. defense posture in the past few years. Insofar as Vietnam expenditures delay or lessen investment available for the domestic needs outlined in this report, those needs become all the more ripe for investment when funds become available. Hence, there is no reason to believe that upon the termination of hostilities in Vietnam the problems of adjustment to measures of disarmament will differ in any significant way from what they have been during the period of this report. Consequently, this report concentrates on the baseline economic conditions which can be expected to be influenced by future arms limitations, without specific regard to special Vietnam expenditures, except insofar as they might contribute to a somewhat higher, essentially short-lived plateau from which cutbacks of funds and effort would begin.

prehensive efforts to redeem "the other America." Americans are also sensitive to the needs of other peoples around the world for economic and technical assistance and are willing, as their readiness over the last two decades demonstrates, to aid in fostering the economic and social development of emerging nations. Meanwhile, the shores of outer space beckon to man's daring and his growing technical capabilities, and the United States has undertaken to achieve pre-eminence in that boundless sea as well.

All these tasks, and more, clamor for a share of American resources. For all their magnitude and diversity, these resources will clearly strain in the decade ahead to strike a balance with projected needs. Despite the magnitude of wealth likely to be available, the total annual cost of achieving a reasonable set of national goals in 1975 will exceed the Gross National Product in that year by approximately $150 billion, or 15 per cent of GNP, according to a recent study by the National Planning Association.[2] Thus, a long view of the future makes clear what preoccupations of the present may only suggest: that hard choices in using limited national resources loom on the horizon for the 195 million people who today bear the most extensive burdens the world has ever known.

Against this background, the readiness, the capacity and the opportunities of the American economy to adjust to measures of disarmament must be assessed. Following World War II, the Korean emergency, and 1961-63 rationalization of the defense posture, the economy moved to lesser levels of defense expenditures and increased emphasis on civilian goals, though in each case the problems of adjustment and the achievements differed significantly. During the coming decade, there is every reason to expect that security requirements, whatever the national government determines them to be, can and will be met, though at a continuing diversion of resources from important alternative national goals. On the other hand, could security requirements be satisfied through reduced expenditures, there are more than enough priority tasks to absorb the resources that might thus be freed.[3] Consequently, if and to the extent that international conditions permit reductions in the American defense budget, the American economy has both the flexibility and the targets to flourish in a more peaceful world.

How that transition might come about is the subject of this report, with particular emphasis on the redeployment of a specially significant American resource, the scientists and engineers whose ingenuity underlies the dynamism of the modern American economy. Although the number of scientists and engineers in the United States is small (1.4 million) in proportion to the overall labor force (78.3 million), their contribution to national objectives is, as in all modern societies, vastly out of proportion to their numbers. From the very beginning of the existence of the United States as a nation, the utilization of technology has been a common characteristic of American economic and social growth, in manufacturing, in transportation, and in agriculture, to name a few areas of special dependence. But the rise of scientists and engineers to special prominence in the United States has occurred only relatively recently, principally within the last quarter century, originating in the need for research and development in support of national security. However, the motivation of defense has never been more than the leading edge of the nation's increasing dependence on the fruits of science and technology. A formal commitment to achieving rapid and balanced progress in science and technology, grounded in the creation of the National Science Foundation after World War II, has ripened into constantly broadening programs of Federal Government support for science and education. Organized sponsorship of research and development by industrial firms, originated in the 19th century, has also increased significantly. The products of this marriage between science and the economy lie in the complexity and potency of goods and services for both the military and civilian markets and in the key role now played by American scientists and engineers in the work of governments — Federal, State, and local —, of industries, educational institutions, and communities.

If "peace breaks out," and the mix of motivations for the accomplishment of scientific and technological activities consequently changes, the impact on the lives and activities of American scientists and engineers will clearly be responsive to such change in motivation. Four alternative levels of defense activity are envisioned as broad assumptions that set the context for the analysis of this report:

(1.) The maintenance of defense expenditures at the level at which they stood at the oubreak of increased hostilities in Vietnam, i.e., roughly 50 billion dollars a year, under which level there would be continuing selective modernization of defense forces, but no rapid procurements of major new weapons systems;[4]

(2.) A *gradual* decline in total defense expenditures from pre-Vietnam levels of about 25 per cent over a five-year period, as was forecast by former Deputy Secretary of Defense Roswell L. Gilpatric,[5] resulting from improving relations between states but no major arms control agreement;

(3.) An *immediate* reduction in overall expenditures, but one essentially no greater than would be involved in the ultimate Gilpatric level, as a result of a negotiated freeze on the production of strategic delivery vehicles;[6] and

(4.) An across-the-board 30 per cent cut in specified armaments, coupled with a verified freeze on all production except for authorized replacements, as outlined by the United States for Stage One in its proposals for General and Complete Disarmament to the Eighteen Nation Committee on Disarmament, April 18, 1962.[7]

These four parameters conform in broad outline to distinct levels of foreseeable restraint and reduction in international tensions. They also suggest distinct levels of impact on the American economy and, consequently, on research and development. In the first case, a foretaste of which was felt in the modest reductions of the defense budget during 1964 and 1965, major new R&D programs and sources of employment would be limited and expansion curtailed in the defense-induced demand for scientists and engineers. Under the second and third set of alternatives, all procurement of strategic weapons systems — or essentially all procurement, depending on political decisions — would be stopped. Research and development of new strategic weapons would be likely to diminish accordingly, either immediately, or as a result of continuing mutual confidence and demonstrated feasibility of mutual self-restraint. In Stage One of General and Complete Disarmament, essentially all major defense-oriented technical activity would halt, except perhaps for the continuation of some research on a stand-by basis, so long as necessary.

In this report, some attention will be given to the

specific consequences for American scientists and engineers that would flow were the circumstances represented by these parameters to occur. These alternatives, however, are mentioned principally as varying indicators of the scale and intensity of the changes in defense procurement that would result from typical measures of arms restraint and limitation. Study and research in the United States has tended to concentrate on the drawing of broad profiles of the impact of such arms reductions and defense shifts on the economy, identifying problem areas, areas of opportunity for the shift of resources, and the range of public and private choices that can be anticipated. Specific projections have been avoided,[8,9] perhaps because of the artificiality of formulating assumptions as to when negotiated arms control agreements might occur and the consequent difficulty of making specific projections as to the scope and economic environment in which specific agreements will operate. There are, however, interesting and useful studies of past adjustments to defense shifts and cutbacks, and of the broad problems that can now be anticipated for specific industries and communities. In recent years, especially with the formation of the U.S. Arms Control and Disarmament Agency in 1961, there has been constant speculation about and growing readiness for meeting the problems of economic and social adjustment that can be expected to occur in the event of defense shifts or cutbacks. Hence, while estimates of the impact of specific measures along the possible continuum of arms control agreements are hard to come by and not especially reliable, there is a wide and growing volume of research in the United States to support a general discussion of the nature of the problems of adjustment and reallocation that would result from limitations in armaments. Moreover, the range of alternative policies of the United States Government has been widely discussed, and a fair consensus has developed among the Congress and the public regarding the basic steps that would be required were international conditions to permit a significant arms reduction.

This report will concentrate on describing in broad terms the scale of current involvement of scientists and engineers in defense work, identifying their distribution by industry and by community. The problems of industries, communities, educational institutions and individuals — as well as governments — will be discussed, and attention will be given to the targets toward which scientific and technical resources freed by arms limitation might be directed. A concluding chapter will assess the readiness of the American economy to undertake shifts in resources from defense to civilian purposes.

CHAPTER I

SCIENCE, DEFENSE AND
THE AMERICAN ECONOMY

BY ANY measure, defense is a major claimant on American resources, both of money and of men. For most of the last two decades, defense expenditures have constituted more than half of the Federal Budget. Increasingly, the purchase of goods and services for defense has come to rely upon scientific and technical research and development to underpin the design and production of weapons. Through the mechanisms of contracts and grants to private institutions — corporations and universities — the Federal Government has underwritten the cost of most of this research and development needed for defense purposes. The result has been intense mutual involvement between the Federal Government and American scientists and engineers in which the procurement of research and development for national security purposes plays a major role.

While the statistics indicate the magnitude of this mutual dependence, they must be heavily qualified to be properly understood. First of all, it must be emphasized that the conduct of science in the United States is by no means wholly dependent upon government support; that other motivations aside from national security and other agencies aside from the Department of Defense *(DoD)*, the Atomic Energy Commission *(AEC)*, and the National Aeronautics and Space Administration *(NASA)* support science and technology; and that much of the work done under defense-motivated sponsorship, especially basic research, would warrant and would probably receive public support for other purposes and from other Federal agencies were the defense motivation not present. As will be demonstrated subsequently, motivations other than defense and sources of sponsorship other than the defense agencies of the Federal Government stand ready to absorb at least a significant part of the slack resources of scientific and engineering talent freed by an arms cutback in the light of the magnitude of accumulated unsatisfied needs in American society that research and development resources could serve. But this conclusion is by no means inexorable, for it assumes adequate compensatory public policies to maintain aggregate demand for goods and services and the readiness of the society as a whole to channel its unique inventive resources to achieve particular nondefense objectives. So while the dependence of science on defense may be intense, it is not total. Moreover, the linkage appears to be sufficiently elastic to justify the conclusion that there exists a high degree of potential transferability between defense and other potential goals and sources of sponsorship for American science and technology that requires only opportunity and determination to make real.

1. DEFENSE AND THE ECONOMY

During the past decade, Federal expenditures on

goods and services in the combined defense, space and atomic energy fields have amounted to about 9-10 per cent of the gross national product (see Tables 1 and 2) and 85-90 per cent of total Federal purchases of goods and services. About 6.6 million persons (more than 9 per cent of the nation's labor force) are engaged in defense and defense-related activities, 2.8 million as civilians in private industry, about a million as civilians employed by the Department of Defense, and the remainder in the armed services.

Defense* work is heavily concentrated in certain key industries. Five categories of manufacturing industry are estimated to be dependent primarily on the production and sale of defense goods to the Federal Government (see Table 3). In all, these five industries, in which employment at the end of 1965 totalled about 1.8 million, employ about half of the civilians in pri-

---

*The problem of distinguishing between closely interrelated defense and non-defense research and development expenditures raises complex semantic difficulties, which must be kept in mind in considering the discussion and the statistics used in this report. Virtually all "defense" work in the United States is carried out under the sponsorship of three Federal Government agencies — the Department of Defense, NASA, and AEC. Not all the activities of these agencies, however, are strictly "defense" in nature. Almost one-half of the expenditures of the AEC is devoted to such non-defense activities as research and development for civilian nuclear power reactors and the Atoms for Peace program. (See Table 2, footnote 4.) The work of NASA serves many objectives, only some of which are related to national security. As the Committee on the Economic Impact of Defense and Disarmament took pains to emphasize: "Certain major programs — principally in space and, to a lesser extent in atomic energy — are by nature not directly sensitive to shifts deriving from defense-related considerations and *may actually be areas of opportunity for increased investment in the event that new resources are avail-*

(Continued on next page)

TABLE 1. DEFENSE, SPACE AND ATOMIC ENERGY BUDGET
EXPENDITURES OF THE FEDERAL GOVERNMENT AND RELATION
TO GNP, 1945-65

Fiscal Year	Amount (billions of $S)	Per Cent of GNP
1945	81.3	37.2
1946	43.3	21.4
1947	14.4	6.4
1948	11.8	4.8
1949	13.0	5.0
1950	13.1	5.0
1951	22.5	7.2
1952	44.1	13.0
1953	50.5	14.0
1954	47.1	13.0
1955	40.8	10.8
1956	40.8	10.0
1957	43.4	10.0
1958	44.3	10.1
1959	46.6	10.0
1960	46.1	9.3
1961	48.2	9.5
1962	52.4	9.7
1963	55.3	9.7
1964	58.4	9.7
1965	55.2	8.6

Source: *Report of the Committee on the Economic Impact of Defense and Disarmament,* July 1965 (Washington U.S.G.P. O., 1965) p. 9.

―――――

able." (*Report of the Committee on the Economic Impact of Defense and Disarmament,* page 5, footnote 1, emphasis added.) Consequently, this report will strive for some precision in its use of the terms "defense" and "defense-related" in connection with statistical data, while the term "defense," when broadly applied, will denote the defense, space, and atomic energy fields as a whole without further distinction among objectives and motivations.

TABLE 2. ADMINISTRATIVE BUDGET EXPENDITURES FOR NATIONAL DEFENSE AND SPACE FUNCTIONS, FISCAL YEARS 1954-1955
(Millions of dollars)

Function	1954	1955	1956	1957	1958	1959	1960	1961	1962	1963	1964	1965[1]
National defense & space	47,076	40,769	40,794	43,444	44,323	46,628	46,092	48,238	52,360	55,307	58,352	55,237
National defense	46,986	40,695	40,723	43,368	44,234	46,483	45,691	47,494	51,103	52,755	54,181	50,143
DoD, military[2]	43,955	37,823	38,403	40,788	41,258	43,563	42,824	44,676	48,205	49,973	51,245	47,382
Defense-related activities[3]	1136	1015	669	590	709	379	244	104	92	24	172	137
Atomic energy[4]	1895	1857	1651	1990	2208	2541	2623	2713	2806	2758	2765	2624
Space research and technology[5]	90	74	71	76	89	145	401	744	1,257	2,552	4,171	5,094

[1]Preliminary expenditures released July 21, 1965.

[2]Includes military assistance.

[3]Includes stockpiling of strategic and critical materials, expansion of defense production, Selective Service System, and emergency preparedness activities.

[4]Includes the following expenditures (in millions of dollars), which Atomic Energy Commission considers for nondefense purposes: 1954, 72; 1955, 163; 1956, 243; 1957, 361; 1958, 358; 1959, 524; 1960, 579; 1961, 665; 1962, 768; 1963, 814; 1964, 910; 1965, 1293; 1966, 1193. The budget expenditure figures shown in this table include expenditures for cost of operation for facilities and for plant and equipment.

[5]National Advisory Committee for Aeronautics prior to 1959 and National Aeronautics and Space Administration thereafter.

Source: Corrected from *Report of the Committee on the Economic Impact of Defense and Disarmament*, July 1965 (Washington, U.S.G.P.O.), p. 76; figures drawn from Treasury Department, Bureau of the Budget, and Atomic Energy Commission.

vate industry involved in defense work. These industries
accounted for about 6 per cent of the total wage and
salary payments in the U.S. in 1963. Defense work is
the principal business of only a very few firms, however,
some of them very large in size but many that are
relatively small.

Defense work is also concentrated in particular,
wide-spread geographical areas. As indicated by the
Committee on the Economic Impact of Defense and
Disarmament *(the Ackley Committee)* which reported to
the President in July 1965 on the prospects for a successful adjustment to defense shifts and cutbacks:

> Among the areas proportionately most affected are the Far
> Western States of Alaska, California, Hawaii, and Washing-
> ton; the Middle Atlantic States of Maryland and Virginia —
> and also the District of Columbia; certain New England
> States, notably Connecticut and Massachusetts; some of the
> less populous Mountain States, such as Arizona, New Mexico,
> and Utah, where the Government's defense operations loom

TABLE 3. IMPACT OF DEFENSE AND DEFENSE-RELATED EXPENDITURES
ON EMPLOYMENT IN FIVE PRODUCTION INDUSTRIES, 1963

Industry	Share of Total Employment in Defense Work	Total Defense Employment in Industry, 1963
Aircraft and parts	9/10	585,000
Ship and boatbuilding and repair	6/10	85,000
Communications equipment electronic components	6/10	445,000
Ordnance and accessories (including missles and space vehicles)	practically all	270,000
		1,385,000

Source: Compiled from *Manpower Report of the President,* March
1965 (Washington, U.S.G.P.O., 1965) pp. 61-2

large; and some of the Southern and Border States where there are numerous military installations, such as Alabama, Georgia, Kansas, and Oklahoma.[10]

As a result, in 11 states and the District of Columbia wages and salaries paid by the major defense-related industries and Federal defense agencies in 1963 exceeded 9 per cent of the total wages paid. In 12 states, mostly industrial areas with extensive and diverse industrial bases, a total of 66 per cent of the national defense-related payroll was disbursed. There are several communities with heavy defense-related industrial or governmental activities, notably Los Angeles-San Diego, California; Seattle, Washington; the District of Columbia; Boston, Massachusetts; Wichita, Kansas; Huntsville, Alabama; and Cape Kennedy, Florida, and several other smaller communities with very substantial defense activities. Some areas, such as the West Coast, are proportionally more heavily committed to aerospace activity, while the principal defense activity of other manufacturing centers, such as the Midwest, is in more conventional armaments production.

These statistics inevitably suggest that major reductions in defense expenditures will have major impacts not only on incomes and employment in the country as a whole, but, more particularly, on certain heavily "impacted" industries and regions. The extent and character of this sectional and regional dependence will govern the flexibility of the economy as a whole, and of these specific components within it, to adjust to changed circumstances and objectives.

2. SCIENCE AND DEFENSE

In the five defense-oriented industries mentioned above, the proportion of "nonproduction" workers — engineers, scientists, technicians, highly skilled craftsmen and professional workers — to all workers in those industries was 43 per cent in 1964, 14 per cent higher than for manufacturing industries in general. In the heavily defense-impacted industries of ordnance and accessories and aircraft and parts, the proportions of scientists and engineers to all workers (in 1962) were 18 per cent and 13 per cent respectively, compared to around 2 per cent throughout the non-agricultural sector of the economy. The five industries employ one-fourth of all scientists and engineers in the U.S. industry and more than two-fifths of those primarily engaged in research and development. These employment figures are hence graphic measures of the dependence of defense procurement upon the work of scientists and engineers.

Other measures emphasize the preponderant involvement of the Federal Government in the sponsorship of research and development throughout the country, and the lion's share of such Federal support that is motivated by defense. In Fiscal Year 1964, the Federal Government spent 15 billion dollars for research and development, almost two-thirds (66 per cent) of the national total from all sources. Of this $15 billion, $13.4 billion was provided by the three defense-oriented agencies ($7.7 billion, DoD; $4.2 billion, NASA and $1.5 billion, AEC), constituting about 58 per cent of the national R&D total. These three agencies sponsored more than half the research and development performed in industry, and 60 per cent of all research and development done in universities and other nonprofit private institutions. In all, 350,000 scientists and engineers, one out of every four in the country, were employed in industry, universities, nonprofit institutions and government on a full-time basis (or its equivalent) on work connected with defense. It should be noted, however, that the bulk of these scientists and engineers were not utilized in research and development but in the management, administration, sales and production phase of industrial activity that would be associated with *any* product, military or civilian, involving a high technological content.

Federal sponsorship of research and development over a quarter of a century has thus increased about 200 times, from a starting point of only $74 million in 1940, and the costs of defense have accounted for a preponderant part of that increase. But the quantitative magnitude of that explosion in support takes on more modest dimensions in any close examination of what these expenditures procure. First of all, it should be noted that Federal expenditures for research, outside of DoD, constituted a total of $7.3 billion, almost one-half of the Federal total, expended by both domestic agencies for wholly civil purposes and by NASA and the AEC for mixed purposes that are by no means wholly defense-related. Such non-DoD research and development expenditures, incidentally, had increased 150 times in the same 25-year time period (from $48 million in 1940), indicating a growing concern of the Federal Government as a whole with science and technology. Moreover, about a billion dollars of the Department of Defense expenditure annually support basic research, whose undertaking is considered to have some utility to defense purposes but also extends throughout the economy. Consequently, while the magnitude of defense support for American science and technology cannot be underestimated, there can be little doubt that much of what the defense dollar procures is no less relevant to the civilian economy simply because it is procured by the Department of Defense.

The priorities currently assigned by Americans to

national security dictate that the performance of much scientific and technical work be undertaken at the behest of the agencies of the government that are concerned with the nation's security. Scientific and engineering advances in defense, space and atomic energy have, however, included programs of direct and indirect benefit to the civilian economy, such as jet aircraft, advances in computer sciences, improved weather forecasting from the use of satellites, and the use of radioactive isotopes for medical purposes. But as the priorities of the society shift, other motivations for advancing scientific and technical horizons can be expected to emerge with equal, or perhaps greater, urgency.

Since 1930, the economy as a whole has shown a marked tendency to intensify its utilization of technology, as measured, for example, by a five-fold increase in scientists and engineers in all fields (defense and defense-related activities included), while the Gross National Product was increasing by a factor of only three (1963 figures). This dramatic comparison is consistent with the growth of defense support for science and technology, but it also confirms the existence of a similar dependence of the society as a whole on technological progress and is consistent with latent civilian demand for the services of scientists and engineers. Statistics on increasing research and development in private industry sponsored by private funds bear out this inference: From 1957-62, privately funded R&D increased from $3.4 to $4.8 billion, an increase of 7-8 per cent a year. Continuing growth of the economy as a whole can only accelerate this trend. The overall record of industrial emphasis on R&D in the production of goods shows significant disparities among different industries, however, (see Table 4) a fact that in and of itself is suggestive of the extent to which certain industries in the civilian sector could well serve as targets for increased R&D effort and investment.

3. AMERICAN EXPERIENCE WITH DEFENSE CONVERSION

The experience of the American economy following World War II and the Korean emergency suggests an

TABLE 4. IMPORTANCE OF RESEARCH AND DEVELOPMENT
IN THE SALES DOLLAR, 1960

Industry	Amount (in cents)
Aircraft, missiles	22.5c
Communication equipment, electronic components	12.9
Scientific and mechanical measuring instruments	11.8
Other electrical equipment	9.4
Optical, surgical, photographic, and other instruments	6.5
Industrial chemicals	5.3
Drugs, medicines	4.4
Machinery	4.3
All manufacturing (average)	4.3
Motor vehicles, other transportation equipment	3.1
Nonindustrial chemicals	2.2
Rubber products	2.1
Fabricated metal products	1.5
Other manufacturing industries	1.4
Primary metals	0.8
Paper and allied products	0.7
Textiles, apparel	0.6
Lumber, wood products, furniture	0.6
Food and kindred products	0.3

Source: U.S. National Science Foundation, *Research and Development in Industry*, 1960 (Washington, U.S.G.P.O., 1963), page 82.

ability to cope successfully with major reductions in defense spending, if appropriate and adequate compensatory public policies are followed, and major non-defense demands are available to absorb freed resources. Moreover, in the modest adjustments of forces commenced in 1964, although reductions and shifts were minor and the transition relatively short lived prior to the Vietnam build-up, further hopeful experience with the potentialities of the economy for conversion was acquired.

Following World War II, during which defense expenditures accounted for over 35 per cent of Gross National Product, the United States was able to demobilize rapidly and without substantial unemployment. In one year, purchases of goods and services for defense were reduced by 75 per cent, or 25 per cent of the GNP, and 9 million men were released from the armed services (three times the current total of the American armed forces). Yet, despite the rapid pace and scale of these reductions, unemployment in the immediate post-war years was held to less than 4 per cent of the labor force. Business investment doubled from $21 billion to $51 billion (1960), consumer outlays rose from $189 billion to $212 billion, non-defense government expenditures increased from $19 billion to $27 billion, and net exports of goods and services rose from minus, $5 billion to $5 billion. The net result was a decline in real aggregate demand of less than half the decline in defense spending.

The principal reasons for the effectiveness of the postwar transition were summed up in the U.S. reply to the 1961 inquiry of the U.N. Secretary General on the economic and social consequences of disarmament:

> Four principal factors operated within the economy to contribute substantially to its rapid adjustment to the post-World War II demobilization. In the first instance, tremendous needs

had developed throughout the civilian sector as a result of involuntary or deliberate neglect during the depression and war years. Second, consumers and businesses had accumulated a large volume of liquid assets as a result of wartime savings which quickly translated civilian needs into strong economic demand. Third, the end of hostilities made it possible to remove the strain on the labor force which had been essential during the war, and many persons left the civilian labor force (or in the case of veterans, remained away from it to resume education or for other reasons), and working hours were substantially reduced. Fourth, the overall atmosphere of dynamic optimism within the country exercised a very positive influence on the ensuing economic developments.

The process of postwar economic adjustment was, however, also helped substantially by effective governmental policy. Taxes were reduced significantly. There was a very great increase in transfer payments, principally veterans cash benefits and payments related to the veterans training and education program. The net result was that despite the massive decline in defense spending, disposable income hardly fell at all. In addition, a large veterans loan program was established to finance the purchase of homes and farms. Generous and quick settlements were made to businesses on termination of war contracts and, to ease the structural adjustment, war materials and related production lines were speedily cleared out of factories. A policy of monetary ease was followed.

In the aftermath of the Korean conflict there was a much smaller real and proportionate cutback in defense spending (see Table 1), which was met with a much less vigorous governmental program. The accumulation of unmet domestic needs was far less great than 8 years earlier. In the absence of bolder steps than the then Administration was willing to take, the nation experienced a mild recession in 1954. Nonetheless, tax reductions helped maintain consumer spending, and backlogs of consumer and business needs kept up demand for durable goods and construction. As a result, the decline in GNP was actually less than the decline in defense spending, and the GNP by 1955 had recovered completely even in the face of further defense cuts. After unemployment had risen to 5.6 per cent of the labor force in 1954, it declined to 4.4 per cent in 1955.

Alongside these trends in aggregate defense demand, major shifts in defense procurement were underway in the 1950's, with little lasting adverse impact except in a few communities that were especially hard hit by obsolescence of their principal defense industry. The value of production of tanks, conventional ordnance, and commercial types of military hard goods dropped from $11 billion in Fiscal Year 1953 to about $2 billion in Fiscal Year 1957. Since the production resources thus set free were not highly specialized, they were reabsorbed in a growing economy, although a major loss of business in the Midwest was experienced. (In Michigan alone, where 220,000 people were engaged in defense work in 1953, the number had fallen to 40,000 by 1960.) Similarly, in the shift of much defense production from aircraft to missiles most dislocations were temporary. But the fact that many defense producers today have never produced for the civilian market suggests that these production shifts of a decade ago affecting industries then recently converted to defense production, and not wholly converted, may have only limited relevance to cutbacks that might be anticipated in the future.

As Table 1 indicates, there was a reduction of defense and defense-related budget expenditures between Fiscal Years 1964 and 1965 of almost $3.2 billion, bringing to an end a decade of almost constant increases. The bulk of reduction lay in declines in expenditures for military functions of the Department of Defense (principally through base closings and termination of new production of certain weapons, in particular, strategic retaliatory systems) and of the Atomic Energy Commission. These reductions were, in part, offset by increased expenditures for space research and technology. The result was immediately felt in the five defense-impacted industries, though to a degree that was lessened by a simultaneous surge in civilian-based demand. In the ordnance industry employment declined by about 6 per cent; in aircraft and parts, by nearly 5 per cent; and in communication equipment by 6.5 per cent. On the other hand, employment levels rose slightly in the electronic components industry (partially induced, perhaps, by a boom in the sales of color television sets) and shipbuilding. By the end of calendar year 1965, employment in these five industries was running 10 per cent above a year earlier. Reductions in defense work, however, had put a severe drag on the growth of employment in some states, notably in the West and Northeast, and in some states unemployment actually increased.

The 1964-65 retrenchment created some concern in the economy about the strength of defense markets, which continued strong civilian demands helped abate. Nonetheless, that brief jolt generated prudent speculation in Congress, the Executive Branch, and in industry about the likely impact of deeper cutbacks. This concern reflected many strands of American opinion — ranging from worry on the part of industry, employees and local governments about the economic health of regions now heavily committed to defense production, to the hopes of those who see as a double blessing the reduction of defense expenses and the freeing of defense committed resources for civilian purposes.

The prospect of cutbacks in defense effort in the

years ahead cannot be said, on balance, to give rise in the United States either to gloomy pessimism or sanguine optimism. Past experience with defense reductions demonstrates that conversion can be successfully accomplished if the Government is alert and new sources of demand are ripe for the application of freed resources. Both conditions today appear to be present once more, although the nature of the unmet needs of American society is such that the responsibility will rest, to an unprecedented degree, upon the Federal Government, in partnership with states and localities, to initiate the mechanisms of conversion and to secure the reallocation of freed resources to civilian purposes.

4. THE MARKET FOR SCIENCE

Until relatively recently, there has been little discussion of the impact of defense shifts and conversion on scientists and engineers, taken as a distinct employment category. Although some unemployment resulted as a consequence of the 1964 reductions, one recent survey indicates that a lesser impact was felt by scientists and engineers than by production workers in the industrial firms most affected by cutbacks. According to the findings of the Aerospace Industries Association, a trade association, total employment in major aerospace companies fell by 3.2 per cent between September 1963 and March 1964, but employment of engineers and scientists dropped less than half as much — by only 1.4 per cent.[11] Despite the limited nature of the sample, this comparison indicates that companies try to hold on to their scientific and technical personnel as long as possible, often using them on company-financed programs and sometimes transferring them to other areas. Scientific and engineering teams, laboriously assembled in a highly competitive market, have a value to their companies that transcends ephemeral softness in the demand for defense goods. This value will presumably remain high, if alternate sources of demand for their talents can be found.

These short-range conclusions are consistent with the findings of Richard R. Nelson in his 1962 study of the broad impact of a 50 per cent cut in the military budget on research and development.[12] On the assumptions that the proportions of R&D expenditures to defense and civilian expenditures nationally are essentially constant and that resources released from defense will be wholly and purposefully reallocated to civilian purposes, Nelson concludes as follows:

> First, that if R&D sales ratios do not change very much, a cutback in defense expenditure compensated by an increase in nondefense final demand will lead to a proportional reduction in R&D outlay somewhat less than half as great. Second, if the ratio of scientists and engineers to total sales does not change in the different industries, a given proportional cutback in defense spending will result in proportional cutback in employment of scientists and engineers about one-quarter as great.[13]

Nelson indicated that defense cutbacks would be likely to fall with the greatest proportional impact on government-owned facilities, next greatest on industry and least upon universities and other non-profit centers, in proportion to the share of the defense R&D budget expended through those performers. In tracing out the consequences of a defense cut on the reabsorption of scientists and engineers elsewhere in the economy, Nelson was guardedly optimistic. Assuming a temporary surplus of R&D personnel and a commercial scramble for new markets, he forecast an intensification of research and development by industry (with salaries holding fairly firm but economies perhaps made in the relatively more expensive support costs for R&D) so as to boost sales via the development of new products. Moreover, the market pressure exerted by the intensification of R&D in some firms would cause competitors to follow suit. Nelson's conclusions as to employment, which assume alert actions by the Federal Government in "oiling the adjustment mechanism," are worth quoting in detail:

> Although scientists and engineers will probably be harder hit by arms reduction than any other occupational group (save military people), it is not likely that unemployment of scientists and engineers will be more than a very short-run problem. R&D is one of the fastest growing activities in our economy. . .; and the employment of scientists and engineers is growing at a faster rate than employment of almost any other occupational group. In recent years, R&D has been growing at a yearly rate of about 6 per cent, while over-all employment has been growing at less than 1.5 per cent. The earlier calculations assumed a given and constant ratio of civilian R&D to civilian demand. In fact, this ratio has been growing rapidly over the past ten years. It can be shown that if the ratio of civilian R&D to civilian final demand does not decrease its rate of growth dramatically, then a phased disarmament program might not reduce total R&D spending or employment at all, but rather would (temporarily) retard its rate of growth. If the response of R&D employment to changes in salaries is reasonably great, and scientists are reasonably mobile, this suggests that the impact of arms reduction on employment of scientists and engineers is likely to be more a temporary retardation of the rate of growth of salaries than significant unemployment.[14]

Nelson's study was based on the impact on the economy as a whole and the demand for research and development of a 50 per cent reduction in defense expenditures, but it is at least equally applicable to arms reductions of lesser magnitude. It assumed both aggressive government economic policies and the sponsorship of particular civilian-oriented technically-based programs such as will be subsequently discussed. His conclusions offer some grounds for optimism that the American economy is sufficiently flexible to absorb limited arms reductions. To so conclude is not to ignore the problems of conversion that reductions will create for industries, individuals, and communities; such optimism assumes, however, the availability of unmet civilian needs for reallocated efforts and the taking of timely and effective public and private action. It is with these topics that the following three chapters deal.

CHAPTER II

PROBLEMS OF ADJUSTMENT

PREDICTIONS of resiliency in the economy as a whole in the event of armaments reductions tend to mask the difficult forseeable problems of adjustment for segments of the American economy and for the individuals whose lives and careers are dependent upon defense spending. This chapter analyzes the nature of these problems as they can be anticipated for industries, individuals and communities that will be directly affected.

1. THE IMPACT ON INDUSTRIES

Americans acknowledge no special commitment to maintaining the markets or profits of particular commercial entities. Despite the dispersal of beneficial ownership of major manufacturing enterprises among increasingly wide segments of the public — including many individuals and groups of individuals represented through pension, investment and insurance funds spread throughout the middle or lower economic levels of society —

the ideology of the free enterprise system places companies on their own to sink or swim as their ingenuity and relevance determine. Companies that have entered defense work have done so with their eyes open to the uncertainties of the field, and they have been fully compensated on a pay-as-you-go basis for their efforts. Nonetheless, such companies are also "businesses affected with the public interest" insofar as they represent proven resources for producing goods and services, major sources of employment for individuals, and tax-paying pillars of their local economies. As the Ackley Committee flatly stated:

> Our national goals do not include the preservation of particular companies, although, of course, we need to preserve a viable group of companies to meet our current defense needs and to provide a base for mobilization in an emergency. If defense firms can successfully diversify or convert the productive resources they presently employ to civilian production whenever the demand for their defense products declines, these firms can and should maintain their present scale of operations or continue to grow.[15]

Table 5 shows the importance of defense and space orders to 34 major contractors in the Fiscal Year 1962, as estimated by Murray L. Weidenbaum. As Table 5 indicates, 17 of these companies are dependent on defense orders for more than half of their business, while others, despite the relatively large volume of their defense sales, would be little affected directly by defense cutbacks. Were all their defense sales eliminated, the Gross National Product would barely be affected. From the point of view of the nation, however, as well as the affected companies, the availability of alternative markets for their resources would help to avert painful dislocations, involving loss of business to companies, loss of hard-won company rights and benefits on the part of employees, and business turn-downs for localities.

TABLE 5. IMPORTANCE OF DEFENSE-SPACE ORDERS TO
MAJOR CONTRACTORS: FISCAL YEAR 1962 (IN MILLIONS OF DOLLARS)

Company	(1) Defense Contracts	(2) NASA Contracts	(3) Total (1) + (2)	(4) Company Sales*	(5) Ratio of Orders to Total Sales (3) / (4) (per cent)
75-100 per cent:					
Republic Aviation Corp.	$ 332.8	$ 6.9	$ 339.7	$ 295.8	100.0+
McDonnell Aircraft Corp.	310.9	68.5	379.4	390.7	97.11
Grumman Aircraft Engineering Corp.	303.6	24.6	328.2	357.1	91.91
Lockheed Aircraft Corp.	1419.5	5.0	1424.5	1753.1	81.27
AVCO Corp.	323.3	1.4	324.7	414.3	78.37
North American Aviation, Inc.	1032.5	199.1	1231.6	1633.7	75.39
Hughes Aircraft Corp.	234.2	9.2	243.4	**	+
50-74 per cent:					
Collins Radio Co.	150.1	3.7	153.8	207.8	74.01
Thiokol Chemical Corp.	178.3	0.8	179.1	255.8	70.02
Raytheon Co.	406.6		406.6	580.7	70.02
Newport News Shipbuilding & Dry Dock Co.	185.0		185.0	267.3	69.21
Martin Marietta Corp.	802.7	1.8	804.5	1195.3	67.31
Boeing Co.	1132.8	15.6	1148.4	1768.5	64.94
General Dynamics Corp.	1196.6	27.9	1224.5	1898.4	64.50
Curtiss-Wright Corp.	144.6		144.6	228.7	63.23

Company	Defense Contracts	NASA Contracts	Total (1) + (2)	Company Sales*	Orders to Total Sales (3) / (4) (per cent)
United Aircraft Corp.	662.7	34.1	696.8	1162.1	59.96
Douglas Aircraft Co., Inc.	365.6	68.4	434.0	749.9	57.87
25-49 per cent:					
American Machine & Foundry Co.	187.3		187.3	415.4	45.09
General Tire & Rubber Co.	366.1	66.4	432.5	959.8	45.06
Northrop Corp.	152.5	1.3	153.8	347.5	44.26
Hercules Powder Co.	181.6		181.6	454.8	39.93
Sperry Rand Corp.	465.6	2.2	467.8	1182.6	39.56
Bendix Corp.	285.9	19.4	305.3	788.1	38.74
FMC Corp.	160.4		160.4	506.5	31.67
Pan American World Airways, Inc.	146.7		146.7	503.9	29.11
0-24 per cent:					
International Telephone and Telegraph Corp.	243.6	2.2	245.8	995.5	24.69
General Electric Co.	975.9	23.0	998.9	4792.7	20.84
Radio Corp. of America	339.6	20.2	359.8	1742.7	20.65
Westinghouse Electric Corp.	246.0	3.4	249.4	1954.5	12.76
International Business Machines Corp.	155.5	12.6	168.1	1925.2	8.73
American Telephone & Telegraph Corp.	467.7	10.8	478.5	11,742.4	4.07
Ford Motor Co.	269.1		269.1	8089.6	3.33
General Motors Corp.	449.0	1.4	450.4	14,640.2	3.08
Standard Oil Co. (New Jersey)	180.1		180.1	9537.3	1.89

* Net sales for fiscal year ending during 1962.

**Not available.

+ Estimated from other sources to be in excess of 75 per cent.

Note: In some cases, it appears that the ratio of defense-space orders to total sales in fiscal year 1962 is not an accurate indicator of the actual ratio of military-space sales to total sales.

Source: Murray L. Wiedenbaum, statement before Committee on Labor and Public Welfare, Subcommittee on Employment and Manpower, U. S. Senate, *Hearings on the Nation's Manpower Revolution,* Part 9 (Washington, D. C.; U.S.G.P.O., 1964), p. 3145.

As long as the defense market is likely to remain strong, however, many firms involved in defense have shown little inclination to turn elsewhere for markets. Until relatively recently, the "aerospace" industry was a "growth industry" in which the potential profit involved in increasing concentration of effort and investment on the production of goods for military and space purposes argued strongly against diffusing or hedging corporate efforts. At the end of the Korean War, that industry was essentially little more than a group of companies organized for the efficient volume production of aircraft; within a decade, however, it became an agglomeration of highly diverse research, development, and production capabilities for producing and integrating a vast array of missile and space components as well as civil and military aircraft. In 1954, aerospace firms employed 48,500 engineers and scientists, but by January 1962 employment figures had risen to about 120,000, of whom 105,000 were engaged in research and development (reflecting an R&D/production ratio unique to the industry); R&D dollar totals for the year 1962 totalled $4.2 billion. By the end of 1963, procurement of strategic retaliatory weapons showed signs of decline.

but Federal expenditures for space were increasing to provide a new field of technology allied to the military market for the products of the industry. Annual Government purchases from the industry remained in excess of $22 billion. The apparent result of this flutter in the market condition was to increase industry interest in exploring new markets, without appreciably enhancing the necessity for actually plunging in.

Many of these firms have never produced for the civilian market. On the one hand, they have, as their research budgets and employment figures indicate, assembled an extensive and versatile array of scientific talent with proven capabilities for designing, developing, integrating and producing systems of vast magnitude and complexity. They have demonstrated an innate capacity to induce technological change, to accommodate to it, and to manage the efforts of thousands of scientists and engineers and numerous diverse corporate subcontractors. These attributes could, under appropriate conditions, constitute an invaluable asset for efforts to innovate to meet complex and extensive civilian needs.

On the other hand, there are also factors affecting aerospace firms that constitute real or imagined blocks to interest in and commitment to civilian production. The industry is oriented toward producing products and systems with a very high degree of reliability, quality control, and advanced engineering. Until rigorous cost-benefit control practices were recently instituted in the Pentagon, these conditions placed an almost preemptive premium on performance. Such products, in their specialization and complexity, are far less relevant to civilian needs than, say, the "jeep" was after World War II; they are likely to be competitive in civilian markets only where extremely high quality and performance is similarly placed at a premium. Research and development for these products, sponsored wholly by the government, is a far cry from the conditions governing R&D effort where the costs must be subsumed by the producer in the end-cost of a product paid for by the consumer in a competitive civilian marketplace. As Weidenbaum has said, "Keeping up with Khrushchev results in a different relationship between supplier and customer than 'keeping up with the Joneses.' "[16] Moreover, R&D on public housing, schools, hospitals, etc., must integrate with a far more diverse and far less firm product environment than is the case in designing weapons for a sophisticated and demanding military customer.

In addition, the bulk of the facilities in which aerospace companies operate has been specially built for defense purposes, not converted from civilian plants as was the case twenty-five years ago during World War II. Many of these facilities are owned by the government and leased to the contractor for specific defense work, so that their acquisition and use for civilian purposes would, under current government policies, be prohibitively expensive. These policies might, and would be expected to, loosen in the event of armaments reductions, but they presently somewhat inhibit the launching of serious diversification efforts. More broadly, there is also reported to be a sense of diffidence on the part of firms contracting with the government about the real or imagined jealousy of their government sponsor over any diffusion of corporate effort away from their principal defense task. This reluctance on the part of companies, whether or not justifiable, is characteristic of the exacting performance and loyalty that weapons production requires and dependence on a single customer permits.

Finally, production is only a small part of what it takes to compete effectively and profitably in a civilian market. Defense firms are oriented toward serving a single customer, who joins with the producer in identifying the needs and objectives of defense products; as a result, these firms lack a marketing structure for civilian products. No matter how attractive a product, in terms of performance or price, it is unlikely to be merchandised successfully in sufficient volume without a structure of dealers and outlets. Aerospace firms lack the dealers and the familiarity with customers and industry consumers necessary to compete effectively with established goods producers. Moreover, the lack of a sensitive marketing structure deprives the potential producer of a proven communication system to perceive customers' tastes and competitors' activities which, if available, would be a vitally important source of guidance for the development of firm and remunerative targets for R&D effort.

Consequently, even if the right product and the right conditions for its manufacture were developed, existing defense producers suffer major handicaps despite their admitted capabilities. A 1964 survey by Arthur D. Little, Inc., a leading management consulting firm, outlined three possible corporate responses to this situation:

> Diversify within the Defense/NASA market complex, in order to sell existing products to new customers or to develop new products for them;
>
> Seek problem areas, in fields other than aerospace, which appear particularly appropriate for the application of the industry's massive technical resources;
>
> Diversify into industrial or consumer products.[17]

The contexts in which each of these three strategies might operate are subseqently discussed.

(a.) *Diversification within Defense and Defense-Related Fields*. The first strategy, diversification within the aerospace market, has already been extensively pursued by the affected companies, as a result of the technological revolution in weapons and space in the past decade and competitive pressures within the industry. As the Arthur D. Little survey reported:

> A survey of aerospace company capabilities brochures and industry buyers' guides shows, for example, that 57 companies claim experience or competence in missile and spacecraft propulsion systems; 40 in inertial guidance platforms; 33 in ground effect machines; 171 in display devices for ground or aircraft; 24 in sonobuoys; 15 in spacesuits (which works out roughly to one company for every two astronauts); and 41 in spacecraft, including all but one of the hard-core aerospace companies.

That observation led to the necessary conclusion that, "There is overcapacity in almost every product area in the industry."[18] There are, therefore, grounds to doubt that aerospace firms can further diversify within the current perimeter of their field, unless major new programs involving extensive R&D are adopted by the Federal Government.

Within the defense field, the development and deployment of an Anti-Ballistic Missile defense is a major new weapons system currently under serious discussion that would generate a spurt of production activity. The deployment of such a system may yet be undertaken, either in a configuration appropriate to defense against a major strategic power or as a safeguard against offensive capabilities from a less threatening quarter. (Indeed, a decision not to build an ABM system along with parallel decisions by other major powers may in and of itself be a foreseeable measure of arms limitation, even while a decision to *build* an anti-missile system of modest defense capability may play a useful role in countering the possibility that an attack by or between minor military powers may be able to inflame relations between major powers.) Surveillance and detection systems which would be emphasized to provide security in the event of armaments limitations are already available, although their capabilities may have to be heightened under a regime of arms limitation, and procurement would surely be increased, especially if other nations, perhaps with the management of the proposed International Disarmament Organization or some entity, were to depend on such systems.

In the space field, as the discussion in Chapter III indicates, major emphasis would be required on such as yet unauthorized programs as a manned exploration of the moon or a Mars landing in order to create new R&D opportunities of substantial proportions.

(b.) *New Problem Areas.* The second strategy, the search for markets outside the aerospace field where the characteristics of the work to be done approximate the unique conditions prevailing in the aerospace industry, has drawn increasing attention from many defense-oriented companies. Among the complex problem areas thought susceptible to the massive systems engineering and program management capabilities of the industry are the fields of urban development—housing, transportation and pollution control; the conversion of saline water and the large-scale use of power sources; and the exploitation of ocean resources. These fields are thought appropriate because they concern extensive problem areas with many variables, not all of which are appreciated in traditionally fragmented problem-solving approaches; major requirements for engineering and technological innovation; and, ultimately, perhaps, the management of large-scale production and even systems operation.

Whether the paper promise of the transferability of systems analysis and systems engineering techniques will prove real remains to be seen. So many barriers exist to the profitability of such work as to make its sponsorship by industries themselves doubtful. Individual companies are unlikely to invest their own resources in major research and development efforts of this sort unless a market for the end product is clearly defined and accessible in the near term. As Michael Michaelis has reported,[19] the market for systems engineering solutions to major domestic problems is fragmented by unrelated political jurisdictions, archaic regulatory practices, and diffusion of the market among many undersized and under-capitalized firms. Confidence in the systems approach is necessary on the part of governments and businesses susceptible to dramatic new solutions. Major and enlightened sponsors for systematic approaches and technological innovation must be found.

Within the past two years, some notable new ground has been broken in harnessing aerospace companies to civilian objectives. The Office of Economic Opportunity, the coordinator of President Johnson's Poverty Program, has called on several leading aerospace companies to assist in the administration of the training centers of the Job Corps, in which youth from underprivileged backgrounds, often otherwise unemployable, are given remedial training in skills for civilian economy. At one such center, Camp Kilmer, New Jersey, the International Telephone and Telegraph Company — whose aerospace experience included personnel staffing for the operation of isolated military radar stations above the

Arctic Circle — has undertaken to train more than 2100
young men. Whatever the benefits of the experiment
will prove to be,[20] Republican critics in Congress have
noted that, at $10,000 per year, it costs more to train a
Job Corpsman than to "send a boy to Harvard." In
terms of the costs to society that such training may help
to avert, the expense may be wholly warranted.

A more orthodox, but no less imaginative, pilot effort has been undertaken by the State of California in
seeking to solve some of its own pressing problems
through the talents of one of its own major, and potential-
ly vulnerable resources, the aerospace companies that
are heavily concentrated in the southern part of the
state. In November 1964, Governor Brown convened a
Panel on Aerospace and Electronics Industries, which
recommended the allocation of $100 thousand for each
of four studies to be performed on behalf of the State
by California industries. Six-month studies were subsequently undertaken to develop broad guidelines for the
establishment of a total system to manage waste disposal from air, land, and water; to appraise the nature,
scope, and problems of the prevention and control of
crime and delinquency; to examine the needs of State
government agencies for a coordinated approach to information gathering, processing, storage, and retrieval;
and to prepare a program for an integrated intra-State
land, sea, and air transportation network.

Fifty-one California corporations submitted bids, and
the successful bidders more than matched the State
funds made available for the work with their own
funds. Although difficult problems of communications
developed between the contractors and "professionals"
in the fields affected, and the information systems re-

port (in a field most closely allied to the contractor's basic capabilities) appeared to have the most ready acceptability, each report offered a fresh and sometimes inspiring approach to a traditional problem area. The report on crime and delinquency, if available a year earlier, might have contributed to identifying the Watts area of Los Angeles as an area for major public concern. (Long following the report's availability, however, only miniscule progress had been made in meeting the stubborn problems of the area it singled out for special concern.)

Each of the studies, by omission, highlighted the problems their approach was designed to outflank: the problems of human, social and political interaction that are not readily quantifiable and that can yield to systematic solutions only when consensus is reached as to their "ripeness" for major and coordinated effort. As a result, the likelihood of the implementation of the California studies through the stages of sponsored research and development of "hardware" is yet unclear; meanwhile, a fifth study of these problems within a single California county is underway. But the methods of the studies have been widely studied and have attracted growing and sometimes enthusiastic interest on the part of other governments and defense industries similarly situated. As this is written, a bill in Congress, introduced by Senator Nelson, would enable the U.S. Secretary of Labor to launch a similar program of regional studies on a nationwide basis of similar problems and of welfare, education, unemployment, and housing.

Nonetheless, however novel the approach of the California studies, some reservations must be noted about the capabilities of the experiment to serve as a model for the salvation of either the aerospace companies or of society. From the point of view of the companies, research and analysis in public domestic problems is not profitable and apparently not capable of usefully employing large numbers of scientists and engineers now engaged in defense work; one contractor reports that 47 per cent of its professional personnel committed to the project were neither scientists nor engineers. Major employment potentials will only be realized if massive technological solutions are actually undertaken, and, even then, the capability of R&D-oriented companies to do more than manage production is doubtful. Meanwhile, skepticism has also been voiced by professionals now engaged in public domestic problems about the degree to which systems analysis and/or the aerospace companies can be effectively utilized. Typical objections are to the "myth of omni-competence" of scientists and engineers and their lack of perception of the subtleties of traditional sociological problems; such objection usually acknowledges no more than a "gimmick" value to systems analysis for calling attention to other-than-technical problems. More-over, there also appears to be some ideological opposition to "encouraging companies to make a profit" from designing and operating projects to help, among others, the poor. Nonetheless, the unchallenged success of systematic approaches in such technologically advanced and functionally integrated fields as the communications industry remains as a tantalizing inspiration to further applications.

(c). *New Product Development.* The third diversification strategy for the aerospace industry mentioned above, the production of industrial and commercial products, is by no means a new concept, but one that has been intermittently attempted by defense firms of all sorts since World War II. After the War, the aircraft industries experimented with a variety of civilian products, either on their own, as subcontractors for established producers, or through subsidiaries. Many used their accumulated earnings to acquire and seek to invigorate other industries, a parallel with only indirect impact on the immediate utilization of the defense firm's own resources. In general, the overall performance was disappointing in the years immediately following the war, as measured by a $50 million net loss of the twelve major airframe producers between 1946 and 1948.[21]

Not all the efforts to diversify into new products have proved disappointing, however. In 1946, Grumann Aircraft sought to capitalize its versatility in aluminum handling to enter the field of small boats and canoes, and later acquisitions expanded into fibreglass boats and hydrofoils. Lockheed Aircraft Corporation entered the shipbuilding industry in 1958 with the acquisition of the Puget Sound Bridge and Dry Dock Company and the building industry in 1960 with the establishment of an Architectural Products Division to manufacture aluminum sidewall for large buildings. Lockheed, North American and Northrop Aviation have all entered the aluminum curtain wall field. Also, there has been, of course, a continuing record of success by defense aircraft companies in the manufacture of products for civilian consumers highly similar to its military production, such as commercial jet aircraft. For the future, the one company that will receive the currently proposed contract for a fleet of fast-deployment logistics ships for the Department of Defense may well expect to attain a position of technological sophistication and leadership from which to dominate the entire shipbuilding industry, civilian as well as military.

Several recent studies sponsored by the United States Arms Control and Disarmament Agency (ACDA) have sought to probe the nature and extent of the diversification problem for defense industry. One study of defense industry diversification by the Denver Research Institute[22] analyzed the experience and outlooks of twelve firms selected for known diversification experiences, geographic dispersion, and variation in size. Defining diversification broadly as the use of a firm's resources to enter a non-defense, non-aerospace business field, by either acquisition or internal development, the Denver study identified real and imagined difficulties in marketing as one principal barrier to successful diversification. Successful techniques for overcoming the hazards of creating entirely new marketing structures were cited — employment of new personnel with commercial experience, association or merger with or acquisition of commercial firms, and sale of services to customers who might ultimately purchase hardware. The study identified the opportunities and drawbacks of two distinct patterns of diversification ("concentric" and "conglomerate") and two distinct methods ("acquisition" and "internal development"). It concluded that the timing of diversification efforts into civilian activities from the point of view of resources and opportunities available to a defense producer is best when a defense boom is *anticipated* (and before it begins), and worst after a substantial defense cutback idles facilities and personnel in defense industries generally. The experience of the 12 companies surveyed demonstrated that, on the whole, given enough resources of management, time, talent, and money — factors insufficiently present in past unsuccessful diversification attempts — new products and markets with sufficient profit potential can be found.

A second report by the Midwest Research Institute[23] weighed the possibilities of diversification for the shipbuilding industry from a principally technical perspective. The Midwest study sought to relate the unique industrial capabilities of an industry clearly in eclipse since World War II to 55 other industries, selected from the U.S. Government's statistical register of Standard Industrial Classifications, whose resource requirements and operating characteristics are most similar to shipbuilding as a whole. The report measured the attractiveness of the conversion opportunities offered by these specific industries by average past and projected growth per year and profitability, the degree of adaptation shipyards must make to enter new fields, and the ability of each industry to absorb released shipyard resources. The industries considered fell into three classes. The construction field, with similar labor, technological, and, to some extent, marketing characteristics, was termed the most compatible, although in that field failures are traditionally high and profits usually low and speculative. A broad range of resources transferable to the manufacturing of fabricated structural metal products, transportation equipment, and machinery was identified, though the profitability of these industries tends to rank in inverse proportion to their similarities to shipbuilding. Secondary manufacturing, the third category, could draw on shipyard facilities of a machine-shop nature. Throughout the spectrum, current labor jurisdictional alignments and conservative shipyard management were cited as barriers to versatile conversion. For the 55 industries examined, 150,000 new job openings annually were forecast resulting from economic growth, as against the 40,000 reduction in shipyard employment that a one-third cut in defense spending would generate.

Perhaps the most comprehensive industry profile of the three studies was a survey by the Battelle Memorial Institute, *Implications of Reduced Defense Demand for the Electronics Industry*[24] in which the characteristics of the electronics industry were analyzed, implications of three alternative defense cutbacks traced out, and a guide to planning for cutbacks presented for government, industry, and communities. With an average of 60 per cent of the industry's sales to the government, principally to DoD and NASA, approximately one-half of the employment in the largest 101 electronics companies is supported by defense work. Defense dependence in the industry is high, especially for research and development (63 per cent of which is funded by the Federal Government), although company funding for research has been increasing in recent years as a result of tighter DoD control of allowable costs, increased performance demands, and a growing civilian market. As a consequence of defense demands for high engineering content and low unit volume production, many small companies have arisen that would be ill-equipped to survive in a more competitive market.

The survey indicated that more than four-fifths of the companies that do some defense business have attempted to diversify, either by developing new electronics products, by marketing existing products commercially, or by acquiring other companies. Their record of success has been mixed, but smaller companies seem to rate themselves more successful than larger companies because of a wide non-defense utility of the components, instruments, and other standard products they produce. Diversification in wholly non-government markets seems to have been less successful than shifts from defense to space production, but some outstanding examples exist of the success of medium-sized firms moving into non-government fields — suggesting, again, that, with enough capital and management drive, profitable alternatives to defense production can be found.

An analysis of "transferability" of companies, systems and functions, technology, facilities, and individuals was attempted, but in inconclusive generality, perhaps inevitable in such a broad-brush study. Approaches to transfer include adapting electronics products devised for defense to industrial use (such as programming devices for machine tool production), marketing new products of another industry developed for special electronics applications in the market of that industry (selling ultra-pure metals by semiconductor manufacturer), and marketing wholly non-electronics products (e.g., children's toys). Both defense-designed electronics systems and functions (such as automatic checkout procedures) were shown to be under-utilized in civilian industry compared to what could be the case if adaptation were energetically pressed. Defense-emphasized technologies (such as display design, solid state applications, propagation, programming and simulation, reliability engineering, non-destructive testing, and remote operation control) were all identified as specially applicable to many non-defense industries, if electronics companies can make special efforts to understand the problems and needs of those other industries. The outright transfer of individual defense scientists and engineers to commercial business, from electronics industries to other industries increasing their applications of electronics products, was thought to offer a "type of conversion with as much promise as conversion of today's defense electronics operations."[25]

The Battelle survey examined the predictable non-defense demand for electronics products over the 1965-70 time period and forecast a continuing annual increase overall of 10 per cent per year, from a total of $8.1 billion to $13.4 billion. This estimate was based on cumulations of an 8 per cent annual growth in sales of consumer products (based on such factors as increases in the sale of color television, home video-tape recorders and sound movie cameras, microwave home ovens and electronic ignitions for automobiles), a 16 per cent average annual growth in sales of industrial products (paced by a 20 per cent annual computer growth rate principally for industrial and sales applications and increases in sales of telephone equipment, especially electronic switching centers), and a 5 per cent annual increase in nondefense government sales (principally to NASA, but also to the Federal Aviation Agency for air traffic control). Against this background of a fluid civilian market, the Battelle study balanced projections of the decline of procurements from the electronic industry as a whole due to various measures of arms limitation:

Assumption 1 — a freeze on the production of strategic nuclear delivery vehicles — would result in a 25 per cent decrease in defense sales in 1 year;

Assumption 2 — Stage One of General and Complete Disarmament — would result in a 73 per cent decrease in defense sales in 3 years;

Assumption 3 — reduced procurement levels (roughly, the "Gilpatric model") — would result in a 25 per cent decrease in defense sales in 5 years.

Its conclusions are set forth in Table 6. Battelle's summary comments interpreting the table are as follows:

The implications are clear for Assumption 3 (reduced procurement). Less than 1000 companies will face any significant problems. A few hundred may have a few years of losses or no profits, and those with a single product line dependent on a single weapons systems would have more difficulties than a diversified company.

The implications of Assumption 2 (Stage I, GCD) are also rather clear. Between 1500 and 2000 firms will have extremely serious profit or survival problems. At least 1000 firms will be vulnerable to closure. However, even with this severe assumption, 2000 companies will have relatively minor problems. One-half the electronics companies should be able to continue relatively normal operations.

The implications of Assumption 1 (SDV-freeze) are the most difficult from which to draw statistical inferences. The majority of the 1260 firms losing 10 per cent or more of their sales in 1 year will be hurt — profits will suffer greatly for that year and perhaps for a few more years. However, it is impossible to determine how many of these companies will fail. Again, it is important to note that 2000 companies should have little difficulty in continuing business in a rather normal fashion.

The Battelle study went on to conclude:

(1) Assumption 1 will seriously damage many firms, but over half the companies will have no more than minor problems. A vigorous electronics industry will still exist.

(2) Assumption 2 will cause hundreds of electronics companies to fail and up to 2000 to have serious adjustment problems.

(3) Assumption 3 can be taken in stride with only minor discomfort by nearly all companies.[26]

The ACDA studies leave no doubt that, however strongly the economy as a whole can be expected to perform, the impact on many individual firms heavily committed to defense work may be very great, depending on the magnitude of the arms reduction undertaken. For those firms with a strong position in or near the civilian market, the impact will be relatively minor, and the conclusion is clear that a firm's heavy in-

TABLE 6. INDICATED EFFECTS ON 3,900 ELECTRONICS COMPANIES PRODUCED BY THREE ALTERNATIVE ARMS CUTBACKS, 1965—70 TIME PERIOD

Percent defense sales (1965)	Number of Companies	Percentage *Decrease* of Sales for Assumptions		
		(1) (one-year period)	(2) (three-year period)	(3) (five-year period)
80 and over %	860	16—23%	52—73%	8—25%
60—80%	400	10—16%	31—52%	8 (decrease) — 9 (increase) %
30—60%	710	0—10%	1—32%	9 (increase) — 35 (increase) %
Under 30%	1930	0—10% (increase)	1 (decrease) —35 (increase) %	35 (increase) — 61 (increase) %

Source: Adapted from *Implications of Reduced Defense Demand for the Electronics Industry*, A Report prepared for the U. S. Arms Control and Disarmament Agency by Battelle Memorial Institute (Washington, U.S.G.P.O.; 1965) pp. 57—60.

volvement in defense work will, even in the state of relative defense stability, be a mixed blessing at best.

But much more research, in depth, remains to be done beyond the limited surveys cited above. The firms and industries that have thus far been studied have been selected more for their accessibility than for their representativeness, and the analysis of skill transferability appears lacking in specificity and depth. Studies must be undertaken of the impact of government policies (e.g., patents, taxes, rental of facilities, cost accounting on defense projects) on the encouragement of interest in civilian R&D on the part of defense producers. The extent of contractor—subcontractor relationships must be better understood. From the point of view of the firms themselves, understanding of the strategies of diversification, especially where mergers and acquisitions or the exchange of personnel may be involved, and of the optimum timing for diversification must be deepened. Attention must be given to the problems of defense firms that must diversify not in luxury, but at a time when other defense companies, with similar capabilities, will be faced simultaneously with the problem of uncovering and exploiting civilian markets.

The complacency of many such defense producers, who tend to discount the likelihood of early or extensive cutbacks in defense production, stands in the way of timely steps to achieve broader product bases and markets during the lead-time that continued high defense procurements allows. It is altogether probable, however, that the drying-up of new defense orders during a period of basic stability or gradual decline in defense budgets (accompanied by a continuing boom in civilian markets, reinforced by growing Federal emphasis on public domestic problems), will — by normal market mechanisms — induce greater interest in and commitment to civilian production, absent and in advance of any major arms limitations. Thus the complacent producer may have something of a reprieve. Meanwhile, all signs point to the inevitability of some severe dislocations in individual firms in defense-committed industries, which alert business managers would do well to foresee while their ability to adjust smoothly is still great. Some business failures must, nonetheless, be foreseen. For companies to fail, that have demonstrated their willingness and ability to serve the public interest, would be especially lamentable—not only because jobs and incomes would diminish but society as a whole would suffer a greater, if less tangible, loss from its inability to harness proven productive talents to satisfy its newly emerging priorities.

2.   THE IMPACT ON SCIENTISTS AND ENGINEERS

To the extent that firms cannot adjust successfully to defense cutbacks, they will be under pressure, as the euphemism goes, "to pass the burden of adjustment on to their employees," i.e., by transfers, reductions in status, and layoffs possibly affecting all except their most key personnel. While historical evidence is scant and not necessarily relevant to future programs of arms limitations, indications are, according to Colm and Lecht, that the "largest proportionate decreases in the event of disarmament are projected to take place in personnel engaged in activities other than research and development."[27] There is also evidence, of a broad sort, that the higher the degree of education and training, the more readily re-employable an individual may be after a lay-off, assuming he is willing to move if necessary to find another job. Moreover, optimism appears to be generally warranted, on the basis of many of the indications cited previously and numerous other long-range forecasts[28] that civilian need for the skills of scientists and engineers is characteristically strong, long-lived, and broadly based throughout the economy.

One little noticed but pronounced trend in the United States suggests in general an increasingly strong market in the years ahead for the skills of scientists and engineers now employed in defense activities. While the number of university undergraduate concentrators in engineering has remained essentially unchanged, the proportion of students studying engineering to all undergraduate students has fallen from 11 per cent to 6 per cent in less than a decade (1956—64).[29] The story is essentially the same for students enrolled in high school physics courses. What this suggests for the not-too-distant future is that regardless of any change in the mix of purposes motivating the work of American scientists and engineers, the margin of demand over supply for their skills in all fields will be significantly greater than it is today. This tendency toward a technical labor shortage will inevitably make scientists and engineers freed by a defense cutback even more re-employable than they would be today. Nonetheless, the burdens of disarmament adjustment will be felt by individuals who, as an occupational class, until now have experienced considerable social rewards for their skill and may be psychologically and economically unprepared for change.

One foretaste of future personnel dislocation was cited in the President's 1965 *Manpower Report*. In the three months following December, 1963, 7700 employees were laid off by the Boeing Company in Seattle, Washington, after the cancellation by the Defense Department of the *DynaSoar* boost-glide missile program. The Seattle Professional Engineering Employees Association surveyed the experiences in finding new jobs of approximately 500 engineers, scientists and mathematicians who had been laid off in the first wave of terminations. Its Report summarized the following mixed experiences:

> For many of these workers, the process of finding a new job was neither easy nor immediately successful. The proportion employed 10 weeks after the layoff was only 60 per cent (117 out of the 196 responding to the questionnaire). And of those who found work, over half had had a period of unemployment of from 3 to 5 weeks. The other 40 per cent of the respondents were jobless at the time of the survey, although most of them had then been without work for only 4 and 5 weeks.

> Of the 117 who were employed, only 20 had found jobs in the Seattle area, and the majority of this group took cuts in pay. A much larger number (nearly 90) found employment in other states, and a few obtained jobs in other parts of Washington. Most of the group leaving Seattle faced the problem of selling their homes, but they were fortunate in another respect. Three-fourths of those who moved to positions in other states obtained higher salaries than they had had while at Boeing.[30]

Despite the hardships of extended unemployment and uprooting of homes and families, the scientists and engineers laid off by Boeing were ultimately reabsorbed in the economy. A comprehensive and detailed study of the Boeing lay-off experience was undertaken by the State of Washington Employment Security Department under contract to the ACDA,[31] omitting separate treatment for scientists and engineers, but confirming the findings of the more limited sample. Moreover, the President's Report also mentioned a shortage of qualified personnel in many fields, especially college teaching, suggesting that jobs exist but may not be matched to the talents of those who would be released from employment.

Personal outlook as well as the state of available employment contributes to the ability of scientific and engineering personnel to adjust to defense conversion. One factor is the state of the current job market, which, as the result of dramatic increases in the demand for specialized technical skills, has resulted in extremely favorable opportunities for scientists and engineers. As a result, the prospect of interruptions in careers strikes with consternation those whose current economic status is often far above their recent origins. For many, home ownership constitutes a significant deterrent to mobility, and others display a cultural indifference to all fields outside their immediate field of work, limiting their initiative and interest in finding new jobs.

Clearly, younger persons — perhaps intellectually fresher, more capable of shifting interests, and psychologically more adjustable — will find transfer and re-employment less arduous than older workers, for whom early retirement may be the solution. On the other hand, many younger engineers have never had the experience of working in the cost-conscious civilian market. On the job training, employee courses, community educational projects, and even further university training will all play a role under company, community, or government sponsorship, as part of a coordinated conversion program to reabsorb their talents. In a humane as well as practical society, programs of assistance in disposing of homes and finding and moving to new jobs will be helpful in overcoming the problems of individual dislocation. Finally, a strong civilian demand for new technologically-based products will do much to create new sources of opportunity to reabsorb

individual scientists into productive, stimulating, and so-
cially useful work.

3. THE IMPACT ON COMMUNITIES

Much as the burden of disarmament adjustment
is diffused when seen from the perspective of individuals, the impact on communities is hard and immediate. Defense lay-offs by a major source of local
employment have a depressing effect on the entire sur-
rounding area, not only on the workers who are displaced, but on all those vendors of goods and services
who depend on their purchasing power, and on all who
hold real property liable to be affected by a wave of
panic selling. Communities themselves will suffer increased demands for services, a shrinking tax base,
and a decline in Federal and state revenues by law
allocated proportionately according to population and the
extent of Federally-impacted activities. Charles M. Tiebout estimates the defense-space generated employment
in the Los Angeles—Long Beach region of California —
composed of direct (via prime contracts), indirect (via
subcontracts) and "induced" employment — at 43.5
per cent of the total area employment. (See Table 7.)
As the Ackley Committee's Report indicated, disarma-
ment-sensitive industry tends to concentrate in many
geographical areas across the country which will feel
the brunt of cutbacks similarly magnified by indirect
and induced relationships.

Geographical concentration of defense industry, resulting from historic factors favoring defense manufacturing (such as the availability of land, skilled manpower, power, and other resources), not only concen-

TABLE 7. DEFENSE—SPACE GENERATED EMPLOYMENT IN
LOS ANGELES—LONG BEACH, 1960*

	Employment	Percentage of Total Employment
Direct defense-space	204,800	7.7
Indirect defense-space	209,800	7.9
Induced defense-space	738,000	27.8
Via consumption	469,000	17.6
Via housing investment	69,000	2.6
Via business investment	58,000	2.2
Via local government	142,000	5.4
Total defense-space generated	1,152,700	43.5
Total employment	2,649,000	100.0

*Footnotes omitted

Source: Tiebout, Charles M., "The Regional Impact of Defense
Expenditures: Its Measurement and Problems of Adjustment," from *Hearings on the Nation's Manpower Revolution, op. cit.,* p. 2519

trates the problem of adjustment, but also creates a
local focus of responsibility for adjustment. But, essential as the initiative of communities to regenerate
their economic base may be, local areas can by no
means handle the problem alone; nor do the ideology
and commitment of the nation allow the problem to be
considered as wholly local in nature. Only the Federal
Government can induce the nation-wide economic
strength, implement special programs of worker as-

sistance and national placement, and, where needed, channel the magnitude of external resources needed to restore the economic base of an affected area. Responsibility is neither solely local nor solely national, but is acknowledged to be shared on a partnership basis.

Community traumas from the decline of business failures, both defense and non-defense, are by no means a new experience in the American economy. What are new, however, are the degree and extent of involvement of many communities in defense work, in many cases after more than a quarter of a century of defense production. Many studies of potential area adjustment problems have been undertaken, but perhaps the most pointed is the recent forecast by the National Planning Association for ACDA of impacts in three diverse metropolitan areas likely to be affected by arms reductions.[32] The study predicted the readjustment problems of Baltimore, Maryland, a highly diversified major industrial city; New London—Groton—Norwich, Connecticut, a small one-industry (submarines) manufacturing region; and Seattle-Tacoma, Washington, an area heavily dependent on one company (Boeing Aircraft Company), forecasting the impacts in each area to be roughly in proportion to the area's dependence on direct defense activity. Alternate assumptions were made as to possible arms limitations — a strategic delivery vehicle freeze, Stage One of General and Complete Disarmament, and gradual reductions.

The results in terms of residual employment losses are summarized in Table 8, assuming a "national offset program" of tax and expenditure adjustments to sustain employment and assist communities and individuals. Percentages in the Residual Employment Loss column reflect special targets for local action to at-

TABLE 8. 1970 PERCENT OF AREA EMPLOYMENT, NEW LONDON, ETC; SEATTLE—TACOMA; AND BALTIMORE

	Direct, Indirect and Induced Employment Loss	Reemployment from National Offset Programs	Residential Employment Loss
New London, etc.			
SDV Freeze	26.0	5.0	21.0
Stage One	40.0	15.0	25.0
Grad. Red.	29.0	5.0	24.0
Seattle-Tacoma			
SDV Freeze	7.0	2.0	5.0
Stage One	10.0	3.5	6.5
Grad. Red.	6.0	2.5	3.5
Baltimore			
SDV Freeze	2.5	1.0	1.5
Stage One	5.5	1.5	2.0
Grad. Red.	2.0	1.0	1.0

Source: Adapted from U. S. Arms Control and Disarmament Agency, *Community Readjustment to Reduced Defense Spending*, A Report Prepared by the National Planning Association (Washington, U.S.G.P.O., 1965), Summary, pp. 15—16

tract new industry in quantities needed for the community and/or increments to the local unemployed. For impacts roughly in proportion to the defense-dependence of the community, the study finds that the effect of "offsets" will be greater on the community more seriously hurt, New London. For Baltimore, civilian space projects will take up much of the slack in scientists and engineers, but not in construction workers, while Boeing scientists and engineers in Seattle—Tacoma will be less able to benefit from space work (which most likely will be transferred to a Boeing plant closer to space centers in the South and Southwest). New London shipyards would be unable to contribute much to either the space program or to consumer or industrial markets, and the community could expect to lose permanently from one-fifth to one-fourth of its total employment. As the study concludes,

> The highly specialized scientific engineering, technical and skilled workers engaged in the research, development, and production of nuclear submarines would have little opportunity to obtain employment in other industries in the New London-Groton-Norwich area if the industry-mix remains constant. . . No choice would exist for these workers but to migrate from the area.

The NPA study emphasized that the greater the warning of impending cutbacks, the greater the capability of individuals, companies and communities to work toward readjustment. Its recommendations for actions by all parties concerned to smooth adjustment will be among those steps discussed in Chapter IV.

CHAPTER III

TECHNOLOGY UNBOUND:
THE NEEDS AND OPPORTUNITIES

THE NATIONAL Planning Association forecast of a $150 billion shortage in American resources a decade hence* uniquely expresses the tension inherent in the scale and complexity of American society. The implications of the NPA study — that imaginative new ways must be found to increase productivity if national goals are not to be trimmed — will test the economy's demonstrated versatility and its capacity for abundance. During the next decade the "promise of the American dream" will seek fulfillment with unprecedented urgency.

Inevitably, technological solutions will play a leading role in the drive to narrow the gap between American aspirations and output. The growth of the economy in the last century has been paced by technological change, which Robert Solow has estimated accounts for 7/8 of the increase in national output between 1909 and 1949,[33] with the balance attributable to expanding capital investment. Since that period, research and development effort has in fact risen at a rate far faster than the growth of the GNP, so fast that only recently hypothetical

*See page 3 above.

(and somewhat facetious) projections of future technical effort suggested that national expenditure on R&D would actually *exceed* GNP by the end of the century. There is, facetiousness aside, every reason to believe that this search for new knowledge and methods — now organized on a more elevated and conscious plane than ever before — will continue at a high and rising level. What that level of effort will be will in large part depend on the priorities for goods and services the society adopts and the policies of government and private institutions to meet these needs.

The resources of scientific and technical skill now committed to national security are thus likely to find a receptive market, should they become available for redeployment. To some extent, that market will call forth the direct transfer of knowledge and techniques now within the defense sector of the economy by conversion of existing productive units. On the other hand, new concentrations of R&D capability can also be expected to form to serve wholly new tasks and priorities of government, industry and consumers. No clear precedent exists for charting such major transfers of intellectual resources from defense to civilian needs, but it is not likely that a sudden or forced draft would be a particularly efficient process. Nonetheless, as the nation becomes increasingly aware of its outstanding agenda of goals and needs and desirous of moving rapidly and effectively to meet them, interest in the unique opportunities of defense technology to serve civil purposes is rising within the scientific community and in the society as a whole. The bases for future demand are thus already being prepared. This chapter outlines some of the areas where technical resources now heavily invested in defense can serve urgent nondefense needs in the decade ahead.

1. IMPROVING THE URBAN ENVIRONMENT

In 1900, 40 per cent of the American population lived in cities, and by 1975 this proportion is expected to have almost doubled. There will be at least 29 metropolitan areas with more than one million inhabitants. A northeastern "Megalopolis" already stretches more than 500 miles along the Eastern Seaboard from south of Washington, D.C., to north of Boston — in which 21 per cent of the American population inhabits no more than two per cent of the nation's land area. Similar supercities are forming around Chicago, Dallas—Ft. Worth, and San Francisco. Central cores are ageing, overcrowded, and inefficient in their use of strained municipal services. Additional pressure, meanwhile, is building up in the suburbs, whose populations are growing twice as fast as the urban cores. The city is hence the focus of the problems of change, growth and adjustment that face the American society as a whole, and the principal field in which they must be combatted. Total national investment in urban facilities in 1962 was $64 billion, more than the total for national defense but less than emerging needs require.

One of the most urgent urban needs and perhaps the single largest aggregate market for released defense resources, is the construction and rehabilitation of more and better housing. As the National Commission on Automation, Technology, and Economic Progress recently reported:

> According to the 1960 Census of Housing, about 6.3 million households with incomes under $4,000 and an additional 2.2 million households with incomes over $4000 lived in units that needed complete replacement. There are approximately 1.5 million new housing units built each year, but population growth, demolition of old structures, migration to other sections of the country, and other losses account for almost all of this

construction. Even if we were to increase construction by
over 30 per cent, a majority of the 8.5 million substandard
units would still be standing by 1970.[34]

Public and private sources now spend more than $20
billion a year for urban residential development, con-
stituting probably the largest single capital expenditure
of individuals as well as the nation as a whole, and the
demand is far outpacing the supply. After more than
a decade of experimentation with a major, Federally-
sponsored urban redevelopment program, the problems
of blight and decay in many ways are worse than ever
before. The renewal effort has been too small in scale,
too diffused in scope, and too uncertain in its goals to
accomplish much more than whet appetites for further
progress. Hopefully, the cabinet-level Federal Department of Housing and Urban Development created in
1965 can soon achieve new perspective and definition
of needs to guide the major attack on stubborn urban
problems that the increasingly desperate plight of
American cities urgently requires.

The costs of constructing adequate new housing are,
however, enormous. At an estimated $15,000 average cost
per dwelling unit, new residences are beyond the means
of those who need them most. Much existing housing
could be rehabilitated, although, if by presently utilized
techniques, at a nearly prohibitive cost and at a rate
too slow to make a major dent in the backlog of unfilled
needs. But the inventive resources of the economy have
yet to be mobilized on anywhere near the scale that
the situation requires and available skills could permit.
In 1960, R&D personnel in the housing industry
represented less than one per cent of the national total.
Moreover, a web of archaic local building codes,
restrictive labor practices, and entrenched commercial
interests in traditional building materials and techniques

holds down the national level of effort in devising and adapting new technology. The market for products and services based on adaptations of new technology is limited and fragmented, and hence the incentives for business corporations to invest the capital and allocate major resources to achieve the needed breakthroughs are weak. As the society becomes increasingly conscious of the need to devise better and better solutions to housing deficiencies, it is hoped that many of these barriers to concentrated effort can fall away, and new solutions, relevant to new definitions of the problems of providing adequate housing, will begin to emerge. In and of itself R&D cannot, however, operate in a market indifferent to its results.

Some limited innovations have already been forthcoming. For example, the use of synthetics such as plastic for pipes and fixtures and bonded aluminum sandwich panels adapted from airplane fabrications. Yet still prefabricated buildings and components account for less than one-tenth of all construction. Mobile homes, which now make up one-fifth of all new housing starts, can be purchased for $6,000 and less, but the mobile home has only limited utility and consumer appeal. Much work needs to be done in improving design, in standardizing and improving prefabricated construction, and, in particular, in achieving modern building codes keyed to construction performance and, hence, compatible with innovation. Economical wide-area rehabilitation techniques must be devised, such as are being sought in one experiment now underway in New York in which multiple dwelling tenements are being rehabilitated by withdrawing debris and inserting prefabricated components through a hole in the roof of the building, which is thus made ready for reuse within 48 hours with a minimum of displacement of tenants. But if one such solution fails, others must be devised and attempted.

Further technical advances can be anticipated in the use of modular wall assemblies with pre-insertion of wiring, automatic devices for handling prefabricated components at the building site, automatic nailing and bricklaying devices, the use of centralized community-wide heating and refrigeration equipment. Experimentations with materials can lead to even lighter structural members and thin-skinned metal clad walls, and perhaps even the use of spun fibres developed for missile shells as exterior coverings, if aesthetic drawbacks can be overcome. Experimental structures molded from plastic and fibre materials have been designed and built and may prove adaptable to markets for houses and schools. For both existing and new units, pre-integrated components are being developed that can be wholly and conveniently removed and replaced as they wear out. But even so, technical capability is a far cry from widespread use.

The successful application of such techniques on a mass scale will require a blend of the systems management and product research and development skills characteristic of defense industry. Computers, for example, can be used to help determine long-range markets and needs for housing and municipal services, to simulate the consequences for a city of alternate urban renewal strategies, to control the manufacturing processes of materials, and even to help create a workable balance in design between aesthetics and efficiency (as in one new curvilinear structure in Washington — the Watergate apartment house, whose nonrepeating details not only delight the viewer but were comprehensible to the building craftsman.) Mass innovation — such as was successfully achieved by the recent California School Construction Systems Development Program under which 22 schools throughout the state were constructed simultaneously with new lighting, partitions, ventilating, and structural systems keyed to specially developed performance standards — could be used for home-building if government action could create sufficiently large markets for innovation. The reluctance of traditional elements of the building industry may also be bypassed by a new Federal program to stimulate similar innovations in the construction of government office buildings by the General Services Administration, with technical help from the National Bureau of Standards of the Department of Commerce. The impact of such concentrated government procurements on the building industry may soon also be further extended by the Department of Defense, if funds are available, through a similar program for building military hospitals emphasizing innovation in design and construction.

The market for materials and techniques so developed will be far larger than the United States alone, since the quest for dramatic new solutions to the problems of decent lower-income housing holds relevance in less developed countries as well, and experience in this field can and will be available for similar projects all around the world. And hopefully the experiences of other countries facing similar problems will be useful to inspire new approaches in the American context.

Housing is but one element, albeit the key one, of the problem of creating more liveable cities. Transportation, health, and pollution control for cities are aspects of broader national problems for which technological solutions will be in urgent demand.

2. MODERNIZING THE NATION'S TRANSPORTATION

As the population expands and the interdependence of the economy increases, the need for modernizing the nation's transportation becomes ever more intense. Within this decade, Americans will probably propel a man with speed and safety to the moon and back, but *not* from his home to his earthly place of work. Traffic jams, crowded airways, and deteriorating shipping and railroads are the consequences of haphazard and unsystematic growth and considerable neglect throughout the past generation. Mobility has always been a key aspect of American life, but mobility has brought with it unparalleled problems as well, not the least of which is an appalling highway fatality rate of 50,000 deaths per year. As the National Commission on Technology, Automation, and Economic Progress recently reported, "Our cities are heavily congested, the trip from home to work is burdensome and time-consuming, the accident toll on the highways is hideously heavy, and the costs of delays in terminal areas are high for all forms of transport."[35]

Many of the problems are clearly not solely technical in nature. Organizational, administrative and financial barriers stand in the way of achieving the broad perspective on transportation as a whole that modernization requires. Railroads are operated according to a pattern of insufficient integration with each other and with the other modes of travel with which their planning and services might well be combined. Some forms of transport are subject to restrictive regulation, and some to beneficent subsidies, to the competitive disadvantage of others. Disparities in performance can be traced directly to a lack of innovative effort; for example, in the highly productive aircraft industry, almost

$4 billion a year is spent on research and development, largely under Federal subsidy, or one-fourth of total net industry sales, but railroads spend less than a fraction of one per cent of their operating revenues on R&D and railroad equipment manufacturers less than two per cent of their sales volume.[36]

Nonetheless, numerous lines for research and development have already been envisioned. Perhaps the best publicized (and possibly least relevant) project is the design and development of a one-billion dollar Mach-3 supersonic airplane, too costly and complex to be undertaken without heavy government subsidy. Considerable attention has been given to the need for rapid intercity transportation on the ground, and the Congress in 1965 authorized a pilot study of the problems of the "Northeast Corridor." Broad design work on the study is underway at the Massachusetts Institute of Technology. and numerous industrial firms have begun their own analyses looking toward product development. The M.I.T. project is not wedded to rail transportation, but is studying all modes that might provide for an integrated system of inter-city transportation at speeds on the order of 350 miles per hour, feeder-lines operating at 100—125 miles per hour, and subsidiary transport with a top speed of 25—30 miles per hour. The integration of the system and the governing of speeds would be accomplished by computer control. Mainline service could be provided by a variety of techniques, including propulsion of vehicles through tubes either above or below ground.

Planning attention is also being given to finding ways of living with the American preference for automobiles, for example, by developing automated guideways, for both turnpikes (intercity) and freeways (intracity), on which individual vehicles would move by a variety of propulsion systems at speeds, where feasible, of up to 150 miles per hour with remote control devices to achieve perfect safety. Electrical propulsion, perhaps through fuel cells technically proven in the space program, or by linear motors or gas turbines, could improve automotive utility and, incidentally, lessen air pollution. Further research is underway on efficient systems for improving the parking of automobiles, and hence increasing efficiency in terms of both driver time and urban land use. Other urban mass transit projects, envisioned or underway, involve passenger movement by use of monorails and conveyor belts.

Further research and exploratory development is in process in hydrofoil and air-cushion vehicle transportation, under both private and Federal Maritime Administration sponsorship, although in many respects work is less far advanced in the United States than in other countries. These transportation modes will not only be useful for high-speed commutation in the U.S., but they have special adaptability to developing countries because they can be readily integrated in rudimentary transportation systems. Developments on vertical-take-off aircraft and helicopters may be limited because the costs associated with these vehicles for passenger transport appear to be inherently uneconomic. Debate is underway about the utility of building a modern wholly automated, nuclear powered merchant fleet, to replace increasingly obsolescent and dwindling conventional ships whose high construction and operating costs have tended to price American shipping out of the world market. Nuclear ships, in particular, offer the prospect of large volume and high cruising speeds, and the uncertain advantage of long cruising times, although as an increment in over-all costs that may not be economically attractive.

Costs and markets loom large once more in determining whether technological promise can be reduced to practice. Integrated planning among transportation modes, already reflected in containerized freight which can move without breaking bulk among ships, trains, and trucks, must be emphasized throughout the transport system. (In this light, a number of contemplated railroad mergers represent an encouraging and perhaps inevitable development.) Further experiments in the range of human factors affecting preference for and use of transportation systems must be pressed. The new Federal Department of Transportation can help rationalize transportation planning throughout the country, and hopefully, thereby, take responsibility for broadening the context of transportation planning and stimulating the necessary R&D.

TABLE 9. ESTIMATED ANNUAL EXPENDITURES NEEDED FOR TRANSPORTATION INNOVATIONS (R&D AND FACILITIES) 1970 AND 1975 (IN MILLIONS OF 1962 DOLLARS)

Mode	Type of Change	Projected in 1970	Expenditures in 1975
Railroads	R&D	260*	330*
Hydrofoils	Breakthrough	375	380
Air Cushion Vehicles	Breakthrough	65	65
Gas Turbine Engines	Breakthrough	750	750
Electronic Highways	Breakthrough	15*	325
Nuclear Merchant Ships	Replacement of Fleet	1020	1020
Supersonic Planes	Replacement of Long-Haul Planes	150*	750
TOTAL		2635	3620

*R&D only.

Source: Lecht, Leonard A. (National Planning Association), *Goals, Priorities and Dollars*, page 183.

Defense industries will hence have extensive opportunities for investment and production in the transportation field, as the NPA's projected cost breakdown in Table 9 indicates, in technological areas on the whole quite analogous to their areas of experience. Whether the conditions for innovation will ripen will depend on the consciousness and joint determination and perhaps the degree of irritation, of the public, of industries both within and without the transportation field, and Federal, state and local governments.

3. MEETING HEALTH NEEDS

Since 1900, more than a quarter of a century has been added to the life expectancy of the American population, but other countries have done better. Recently, the nation has taken on markedly greater aspirations, as is reflected in President Johnson's target proposal to extend life expectancy by five more years within the forseeable future.[37] The passage of a comprehensive health care program for the aged in 1965 represented the first broad step toward public responsibility for improving health care for all. Other recent legislation provides for the establishment of community mental health centers, an expansion in research in the fields of heart disease, cancer and stroke, and increased hospital building. All told, the nation is committed to a stepping up of its efforts to improve health care to diffuse excellent health care more broadly throughout the society, and to bring research results more speedily into practice.

Despite the specialization of health research and development, technology now committed to defense may well have a specially important role to play in the design and application of systems to support the medical doctor and the health scientist. Preeminent in these applications will be the use of computers — to speed diagnoses, to aid in the mass screening of large numbers of patients, and to extend the scope of medical research, as well as to reduce some of the mountainous administrative work required of health personnel. Within the last decade and a half, the ratio of doctors to the population has not significantly increased, and medical school enrollments do not promise significant relief; consequently, to the extent that the work of doctors and nurses can be made more efficient, health care can be readily improved and the benefits of medical knowledge diffused more widely.

In the development of products for defense and space purposes, American industry has vastly increased its capabilities in miniaturization, reliability and automatic controls. Much of this advance may be relevant to the design of artificial organs and to diagnostic and remote monitoring equipment utilizing modern defense-induced advantages in signal processing, pattern recognition, telemetering and remote recording; lasers may become useful for fine surgery impossible by more conventional methods.

Exploiting the capabilities of defense industry will require careful and extensive efforts to steep defense R&D personnel in applications with which they may be wholly unfamiliar, and to make health workers more conscious of knowledge and techniques hitherto veiled by considerations of security or supposed irrelevance.

4. PROTECTING THE ENVIRONMENT

A satirical song somewhat popular in the United

States these days advises the visitor from abroad, "Don't drink the water, and don't breathe the air!" The truth of America's problems of waste disposal is far less grim than that ballad suggests, but it does convey the nation's mounting concern for improving the methods by which the inevitable waste products of its growth and development are handled in the environment. The fields of air, water and soil pollution, and the allied problem of ensuring the future availability of water resources of adequate quality and quantity will draw increasing investments of public and private resources and scientific and engineering talents in the years ahead.

The state of California, containing the nation's largest motor vehicle population, has recently enacted legislation to require the installation of exhaust filtration devices on all new cars, and similar legislation has been passed in the Congress, effective throughout the nation. But such filters will be only partially effective, and more research must be done not only in cleaning up engine exhausts and crankcase fumes, but also in the development of new methods of propulsion such as electric fuel cells and gas turbines without pollutant by-products. Smoke pollution from industrial processes, electrical power generation, and refuse incinerators can also be reduced by improved equipment and the adoption of wholly new heat and power sources. Increasing enforcement of public regulation and improved standards promise to break the pattern by which those responsible for pollution are indifferent to its consequences and to create new markets for control devices and alternate power sources.

Except for a few areas in the United States, water has always been available in adequate quality and quantity; however, expanding population and industrialization threaten to diminish these rich resources. The problems are diverse and widespread. Growing populations, more heavily concentrated in urban areas with increased industry, discharge greatly increased pollutants into streams. In addition, pollution from agricultural chemicals, salts from leaching of soil, and acid mine drainage add pollutants in rural areas, and reduction in streamflow from increased usage increases the proportion of pollutants. Wholly new treatment facilities are needed in many areas, especially small cities and suburbs dependent on septic tanks, making improvements in the technology of water quality management a vital national need.

Despite the ample overall availability of water supplies, the lack of water in particular areas has already begun to impose ceilings on growth and development. Recently the entire Northeast suffered such a shortage that water conservation practices were stringently adopted, most notably in New York City. In the Southwest, where irrigated desert lands have recently experienced dramatic agricultural and urban growth, concern about future availability of water to support increased population is reflected in acute multi-state rivalries for access to and control of waters in the Colorado River. Looking ahead to the end of the century, the Federal Council for Science and Technology recently forecast regional shortages for the Upper Missouri Basin, the Southern Pacific region, the Gulf Coast, and even the Eastern Great Lakes, and a nationwide excess of demand over supply of almost 200 billion gallons a day during years of subnormal precipitation.[38]

Numerous suggestions have been made for major engineering works to be built over this period, the most dramatic of which is the proposed continent-wide North

American Water and Power Alliance, in which the United States and Canada would cooperate on a comprehensive multi-billion dollar water development plan. But the potential market for the goods and services of defense industries in these areas is not likely to include construction of dams and irrigation works, since different kinds of engineering from the specialities of defense firms are required. Less direct opportunities for defense firms will, however, exist: Products ranging from pipes to airconditioning systems not dependent on water must be designed and marketed. Again, since improved management of existing water supplies is a key to problems of resource quantity and quality, the application of systems analysis techniques will be of utmost importance. Several avenues to achieving inexpensive desalted water, including the use of nuclear power in connection with large dual purpose electric generation, are under study, and are nearing the point where desalted water may become economically feasible for some rural and urban uses. The results of this research, to which industries as well as the Federal Government are committing significant funds and efforts, will, of course, be of great value not only to the United States but to a large number of other countries urgently in need of water. Discoveries in the allied fields of meteorology and oceanography, subsequently discussed, will improve knowledge of the hydrologic cycle and perhaps lead to the availability of new tools for water management.

5. METEOROLOGY AND OCEANOGRAPHY

Three major advances have combined to improve vastly the prospect that man may be able to modify weather and climate, with countless economic and social benefits — and dangers as well. Increasingly complete and elaborate mathematical models are being constructed for a variety of atmospheric systems, reducing the inhibiting effects caused by empirical approaches to our understanding of the atmosphere. The availability of high-speed high-storage-capacity computers has made these models meaningful for understanding the vast complexity of weather systems and, through numerical simulation, for predicting weather patterns. Finally, extensive experience with new measuring tools — through the use of aircraft as measuring platforms, through radar, and most recently the meteorological satellite — and increasing world-wide integration in the interchange of weather information have significantly increased the range of available knowledge and data about atmospheric processes.

The results await synthesis, but in the recent words of the National Academy of Sciences' Panel on Weather and Climate Modification, "one senses that already we have available the measurement skills requisite to monotoring adequately many of [the] atmospheric systems we seek to modify."[39] It would be idle to predict more in this field than its basic ripeness for stepped-up innovative effort, of which the fruits, however, would be significant. Even a reliable five-day system of predicting weather conditions, it has been estimated, would spell an almost $6 billion annual savings for American agriculture, water resources, transportation, retail sales, and lumber. Vast areas of the world could directly and profoundly benefit from modifications in weather and climate conditions, and equally from improved long-range forecasting over periods of weeks to months.

Speculative as the long-range prospects and opportunities for weather and climate modification may be, however, the nation's expectations from expanded oceanographic research and development are higher and more certain. An eleven-fold growth in Federal support for oceanography has occurred since 1958, capped recently by the creation of a National Council on Marine Resources and Engineering Development in the Executive Office of the President to coordinate the activities of the more than 20 government agencies engaged in aspects of oceanographic work. Beyond the national security aspects which have sustained a major share of the growing investment in oceanography, benefits are expected from expanded oceanographic research via increases in fisheries production, exploitation of marine minerals, recreation, sewage disposal, improved shipping and long-range weather forecasting. Estimates of useful applications for freed defense resources have ranged as high as $2 billion for operating costs for ships and expansion of needed facilities, including the building of a new fleet of oceanographic ships.

Studies which might be undertaken include detailed exploration, drilling and coring of the continental shelf, the continental slope and adjacent ocean basins, and detailed sampling and analysis of known mineral deposits on the ocean floor. Some areas of the oceans are insufficiently charted, such as the South Pacific, and in other areas much knowledge could be gleaned from systematic measurements of circulation patterns and ocean currents. The interaction of the air and the sea is little understood and should be of special importance in understanding both media. Moreover, detailed studies and experiments of "aquaculture" — farming of the sea — could be undertaken to provide new sources of protein at low cost to meet current and projected nutritional deficiencies all around the world.

The expansion of national oceanographic programs would make possible the ready redeployment of personnel, including scientists and engineers, now engaged in defense activities. An expanded national program would also provide the basis for increased U.S. participation in cooperative international oceanographic undertakings, possibly with other countries whose resources had similarly been freed from military activities. The seas, which cover almost three-quarters of the earth's surface and touch on most of the populated regions of the world, could then become a symbolic avenue for peaceful cooperation and the joint determination of all peoples to improve the conditions of human life.

6. SPACE

The conquest of space, undertaken in part for reasons connected with national security, also serves the broader national objective of increasing our knowledge and control over our environment. The *Apollo* program, by which the United States has undertaken to land a man on the moon and bring him safely back to earth by 1970, if not sooner, is expected to cost more than $20 billion; as such it constitutes the single largest research and development program in history. Wholly new fields of science and engineering are emerging as outgrowths of space research, and new products and processes for the economy as a whole are foreseen as the byproducts of space efforts, with applications in improved weather forecasting, reconnaissance (in support of both negotiated and self-imposed arms limitations), mapping, and communications.

The objectives of the Apollo program are narrowly

defined, and leave room for a host of other applications and objectives for the growing American capabilities in space. As a result, the space program can serve as a target for scientific and technical resources, many of which are now committed in analogous fields of military work, limited only by the new knowledge uncovered in man's first steps into space and by his imagination. Although it would unduly deprecate the objectives of the space program to consider it a "makework" program, it is no less true that justifiable efforts in space exploration could readily take up much of the slack in specialized resource-allocation created by defense cutbacks. Insofar as reduced defense demands would create a surplus defense industrial capacity, current constraints on the allocation of scarce scientific and engineering skills to space work would correspondingly diminish. Consequently, some increase over the $5 billion currently expended on space projects could well be undertaken, with the amount dependent upon the extent to which freed defense resources are needed for other goals.

Major expenditures on the Apollo project are due to decline after 1968, when the bulk of the engineering work will be completed. It does not appear that any commitments have yet been made for follow-on missions, but two prime candidates are the intensive exploration of the moon (which might cost as much as the Apollo program itself) and a Mars program (the initial landing for which has been estimated to cost in the vicinity of $100 billion). Neither of these projects would be lightly undertaken, and they will obviously depend, in part, on the results of preliminary space discoveries as well as the programs of other countries. Perhaps these follow-on missions might well be undertaken, as the United States has proposed with regard to the Apollo program, on a cooperative basis with other advanced countries.

Beyond these principal missions, other space activities will continue in the decade ahead, requiring increasingly sophisticated technological applications. These include orbiting reactors and nuclear-propelled rockets, expanded research with an utilization of meteorological satellites, and increasing exploitation of satellites for communications purposes, by industry (e.g., COMSAT) and government, alone and in cooperation with other countries. Research and development in support of the exploration and utilization of space is only in its infancy.

7. THE CONTEXT FOR INNOVATION

The six areas of innovation presented here are listed principally as illustrative of fields in which American science and technology will be called upon to generate new solutions to pressing national needs. They by no means limit the areas in which defense technology can be adaptable to non-defense purposes. In particular, the thread of potentiality of computers and systems analytical techniques which runs through the areas listed here will have widespread applications throughout the economy, many as yet unforeseen. With continuing advances and increasing supply, computers are becoming faster, smaller and less expensive. Through these developments and the expanding use of shared-time procedures, facilitated by cooperation of the communications industry, computers may soon be available for almost any business of appreciable size. As Paul Armer of the RAND corporation recently forecast for the National Commission on Technology, Automation, and Economic Progress,

> As total costs continue to decline, computers will become commonplace and someday will be found in every factory, every office, every business establishment, every classroom, every airplane, every car, every home, and maybe eventually on every person.[40]

Applications will extend to control manufacturing processes and provide automatic warehousing; to process and manipulate pictorial images and graphic information, for example in the conception and design of buildings; to process and to a limited extent translate language; and to recognize patterns, such as the human voice, or the human fingerprint, the latter, for example, as a universal source of credit. Armer has forecast particularly extensive computer applications for transfers in banking which may rapidly replace the function of bank checks. Governments have already made wide use of computers and data-processing equipment for computations and information storage and retrieval, at considerable cost savings; the ratio of Federal employees to national population has begun to decline, in large part through the introduction of electronic data-processing equipment. Use of these systems will expand in the future, especially at state, local and intergovernmental levels. The publishing industry, already beset with major labor problems, has begun to replace the linotypist and compositor with computer-operated automatic typesetting machines. The use of these machines will doubtless displace many workers with obsolescent skills (although the demand for others with higher skills will probably increase). There will also be the inevitable and controversial social consequence of reducing individual privacy. Nonetheless, the potential useful applications of computers are legion, providing a wide path for the diffusion of technologies originated in the defense field through the civilian economy.

The prospects for new applications of the computer are enhanced by the even broader potency of the electronics industry as a whole, which has grown and innovated in the last decade largely spurred by urgent defense applications. As Philip Siedman wrote in a recent issue of *Fortune,*

> Integrated circuitry will not only gradually take over existing kinds of consumer products, it will inspire totally new ones. A starter list of possibilities includes inexpensive electronic organs, portable telephones, low-cost video tape recorders, personal paging devices, and remote control switches for household lighting. One particularly attractive candidate is electronic safety equipment for the automobile. Engineers are already thinking about a "black box" that would guide drivers in stopping in the shortest possible distance without skidding, and a radar-like device that would warn the driver whenever he was approaching another car at a dangerous closing speed.

> The market impact of such products could be beyond imagination. Who could have predicted the consumer's love affair with the electric toothbrush? How many people foretold the incredibly rapid growth of the television market and its immense sociological consequences? Now, with a technology capable of packing all of the logic functions of a small computer inside a cigar box, the electronics industry seems once again to be on the verge of radically reshaping our way of life.[41]

Not all the innovations that will enrich or redeem American life can be foretold. One area in which the application of technology and modern problem-oriented approaches is becoming increasingly important, and in which the reemployment of skilled scientists and engineers will be desirable, is the field of education. The interaction of technology and the educational system can be made increasingly fruitful in the years ahead; growing attention is being given to finding ways to make the interaction a two-way street. More than $30 billion is spent annually in the United States for education, but the problems of inadequate teachers and facilities throughout the educational spectrum make the quality of education highly uneven. Increasing attention has been given in the United States both to developing electronic teaching aids and to the process of applying systemically the results of educational research and development — ambitiously defined in a recent study as the process of learning "how to provide for all students what an exceptional teacher provides for a few,"[42] using technological methods as a part of an integrated problem-oriented approach to the teaching process.

More than 100 educational television stations now exist in the United States for home and classroom use, and the Ford Foundation has only recently proposed an economically revolutionary, but technically familiar system of transmitting commercial network TV programs by publicly-chartered satellite, the revenues from which would vastly increase funds available for educational television. Audiovisual equipment (phonographs, tape recorders and films) are in wide use, but much work is now underway on systems of increased flexibility, simplicity and adaptability to the learning-speed and interests of individual students. Ultimately, adaptations of computers may provide each child access to vast quantities of information that can be interrogated simply and can engage him in a dialogue that can be both exciting and informative. Construction of new schools that can be both economical and attractive environments for learning will rank with other construction needs as fields where innovation, as in the California project mentioned above, must be pressed. Meanwhile, expanded emphasis is being given to systematic curriculum reform, beginning a decade ago with the revolutionary development of a new high school physics course, keyed to comprehensive presentation of subject matter according to the most contemporary standards and the individual student's ability to learn, and extending now to other fields of learning at all levels of education.

Beyond the devising of "hardware" and "software" for teaching, individual scientists and engineers displaced by arms reductions may find specially satisfying opportunities as teachers themselves. Not all those that would be affected would be suitable, intellectually or temperamentally, but many could be reabsorbed in the educational system with special training. The growth of the student population, increasing length of study and specialization, and the need for smaller classes for all and increased educational effort for some elements of the student population are creating a major — and somewhat elastic — need for increased and improved teaching resources.

The work of the group of scientists and engineers now involved in the educational system in university research will retain a special importance to both science and education. Despite decline in defense-motivated support, other justifications for maintaining the health of basic research will remain as the key not only to new approaches to familiar problems, but also to the continuing richness of technical education. Strength in research and education, increasingly desired in the U.S. in the past two decades, will be all the more important in a society whose "pursuit of happiness" is less distracted by considerations of security.

CHAPTER IV

THE PROSPECTS
FOR ADJUSTMENT

THERE WILL be problems of adjustment in the American economy in the event of armaments reductions. This much is clear from even the most cursory examination. Those problems will be deeper and longer lived depending on the extent and the speed with which expenditure cutbacks occur. Dislocations are perhaps inevitable, given the magnitude of the nation's investment of resources and people in defense work and the duration of the nation's mobilization throughout the Cold War.

But the conclusion is equally clear that an enormous backlog of public needs — as opposed to the private needs whose solution facilitated the economy's adjustment of two decades ago — presses upon the nation's resources. After decades of constant change and growth, the American people assiduously desire the opportunity to turn their vast productive resources once more to their own welfare. To state this emerging desire is not to predict a readiness to abandon international commitments for the sake of domestic goals, for it is the characteristic of a highly motivated people to espouse sacrifice for the sake of deeply felt purposes. Nonetheless, should national security be achievable by cooperation and negotiation — which many think is the surest course to security in a world armed with nuclear weapons — this country should welcome the opportunity to devote its resources to the renewal of its unfulfilled society.

A strong and healthy economy is the best guarantee of readiness to absorb the resources released from defense purposes. The recent Report of the Committee on the Economic Impact of Defense and Disarmament charts the course of the economy over the second half of the nineteen-sixties with reference to the possible imminence of a major reduction in defense spending. According to the Report, even without such reduction, because of a growing work force and growing productivity, there will be an inevitable requirement for "major fiscal action" — in the form of expenditure increases by the Federal Government and/or a decrease in taxes of from $25 to $30 billion — to preserve full employment and maintain a healthy economy.[43] With a 25 per cent defense cutback from 1965 levels, this target for fiscal action would grow to $38 to $40 billion. By this, the Report means that new purchasing power in these amounts would have to be injected into the economy by the Federal Government to keep demand level with expanding output. Hence, for wholly practical reasons, increased public expenditures and/or increased private resources will have to be made available at a time of rising national domestic needs.

This aggregate readjustment will by no means be difficult to achieve. Major demands upon the Federal Government — from rebuilding cities to expanding welfare payments — ensure growing Federal responsibilities; although major domestic programs have been enacted since 1961, the agenda of "Great Society" legislation is still far from complete. Many of the most difficult domestic problems lie in the traditional fields of State and local governments. Expansions in the grant-in-aid cooperative governmental programs will hence be required, along with the possibility, proposed but yet untried, of direct subventions from the Federal Government to states and localities. Additional amounts could be left within the economy in the form of tax cuts, which would directly contribute to enhancing the purchasing power of consumers, with a rapid impact on civilian durable goods industries. The techniques for fiscal readjustment are by now largely proven economically and politically acceptable, even while the targets for future reallocation are becoming increasingly well defined.

Measured against the background of such fiscal policies, the problems of adjustment of particular aspects of the economy — industries producing finished goods, certain workers and communities — appear limited if no less stubborn. But expenditures will inevitably rise in some areas of the economy while others will suffer a decline as a result of defense cutbacks. Demands for skilled personnel in the health, education, and human welfare fields will rise, and governments will require more personnel with social sciences skills. Some problems of unemployment will result, which early warning of impending cutbacks, retraining, and expanded job placement services can help to overcome. Other workers will be retained in existing employment, if corporate energies can be mobilized to new areas of public needs and a matching of new government interests appropriate to available skills and capabilities can be devised.

To some extent, business failures, unemployment,

and community deprivations will eventuate, but advance preparation and energetic adjustment policies can help minimize these dislocations. Some preparations have already begun. Since its founding in 1961, the Arms Control and Disarmament Agency has been conducting and sponsoring studies through its Economics section, and seeking to generate industry, government and university interest in the problems of readjustment. In the Department of Defense, the Office of Economic Adjustment has had notable, if limited, success in providing early warning and assistance to communities where defense bases have been shut down in finding new industry and sources of employment. Significant experience has been gathered with guaranteeing displaced Defense Department employees jobs elsewhere in the event of terminations, and one proposal would have the DoD underwrite the sale of housing owned by its own civilian employees as a result of job transfers. Through studies and research, the Department of Labor is improving its understanding of the characteristics of the labor market, particularly in regard to worker adaptability, and the Federal-State Employment Service is seeking to increase its now limited capability in finding jobs for scientists and engineers. In particular, the studies of the Committee on the Impact of Defense and Disarmament have helped to bring together the planning of all government agencies, and a government-wide coordinating network now exists on a stand-by basis, for adjustments in the event of disarmament.

Equally as significant as the continued maintenance of a healthy economy will be the continuing enactment and implementation of broad Federal programs to meet the nation's needs for expanded public services. Volumes of legislation have already been enacted under the banners of the "New Frontier" and the "Great Society." In the aggregate, these programs represent not only increasing national efforts to keep abreast of growth and development in the population, but also expanding governmental responsibilities for aspects of the well-being of the American people that cannot be met by the operation of unassisted free enterprise, or cannot be left to the limited and divided resources of the States. Throughout the preceding chapter has run the theme that public wants have not been served because of the fragmented nature of approaches to vital problems; expanded Federal responsibilities are not only concentrating the efforts of governments but creating a market for goods and services that the private sector of the economy can more efficiently serve.

Only by finding new targets for public and private concern can the process of reallocating resources be successfully completed. Civilian purposes as clearly defined and strongly felt as is defense today will be essential to provide the stimulus and the target for technology freed from defense objectives. As pointed out earlier, technology cannot flower in a vacuum, and the productivity of technological innovation cannot in the long run exceed the priority that society is willing to place on the targets that innovation serves. As long as defense demand remains strong, consequently, scientific and technical resources now committed to defense are likely to remain somewhat "sticky" and conservative with regard to wholly new fields for application of effort. But, meanwhile, increasing government investment in civilian needs in advance of armaments reductions can, incidentally, be viewed as laying a modest groundwork for later conversion of substantial scientific and technical resources. To help strengthen that "demobilization base," further steps to encourage a snowballing demand for inventiveness in civilian nondefense industries might well be undertaken — such as tax credits for corporate R&D and the expansion of technical assistance programs to specific "under-researched" industries, but such programs to stimulate R&D cannot transcend the degree of emphasis that society as a whole chooses to put upon particular civilian programs. The best technological contribution to solving the nation's major domestic problems will be secured if and when the society as a whole unequivocally demands their solution.

A pronounced theme of Federal action in the last half-decade has been a growing emphasis on research and development as a vital aspect, with high "benefit—cost" ratios, of public policies. Scientists and engineers have come to play a growing role in government councils, and, as a result, public servants are increasingly informed about the capabilities of technology to meet public needs. This increased emphasis, originally confined to the national security area, has now spread throughout those agencies of the Federal Government concerned with filling urgent domestic needs. The process is yet far from complete, and, as the House Committee on Government Operations recently somewhat acidly reported,[44] the tools and capabilities of the Federal Government to sponsor innovation in the fields of urban transportation, housing and hospital facilities, and water pollution control tend to lag far behind the abilities of the DoD, AEC, and NASA to harness technology to meet their objectives. Without a technically sophisticated sponsor with a clear vision of desired performance, the cooperative process of research and development, sponsored by public agencies but performed by private institutions (corporations and universities), lacks tone and direction. As increasing emphasis is given to R&D in support of national needs such as those outlined in the preceding chapter, attention will have to be given to strengthening the largely undeveloped capabilities of governments, as well as private institutions, to engage in a productive dialogue. For the diffused and fragmented domestic fields which this report has suggested for increased emphasis, that dialogue is in many ways even less advanced than was the sorry state of the nation's readiness for the Space Age a decade ago.

The record of individual states has been even less alert, although the California studies suggest a promising exception. Most state governments possess only rudimentary capabilities — technical, financial, and intellectual — to apply technology to their people's needs, and are largely unconcerned in a constructive sense with the consequences arms reductions might have for their own familiar and preoccupying local problems. As the Federal Government advances its planning for nationwide domestic programs and the states reassess their needs for new resources, methods and solutions, the likelihood grows that when and if arms reductions come about (if not before), steps to meet the problems resulting will be cooperatively undertaken on a Federal-State or multi-state basis.

Much planning and effort is also needed within defense industries, though their preparations for future defense cutbacks will be clearly dependent, in part, on the strength of the signals they will receive from the Federal Government. To the extent that governments — Federal, state, and local — demonstrate their interest and willingness to invest in new domestic fields, alert defense industries will adjust their planning and goals accordingly.

Individual scientists and engineers will feel the brunt of the dislocations caused by armaments reductions. They are by no means destined as a group to suffer dismal deprivation or extensive unemployment, but the loss of creative and promising employment possibilities may well change the lives of many of these individuals whose talents constitute a precious national resource. Many such people have already expressed increasing interest in committing their careers to the dramatic new fields for technological applications outlined in this report. Many have also expressed strong desires to participate immediately in attacking the problems of international economic and social development, but information about opportunities and mechanisms for employing their interests have been lacking.

The foregoing analyses and prescriptions have concentrated on the needs, problems and opportunities of American society for reallocating, within itself, its own scientific and technical resources. From the point of view of the prospects for success of this yet-to-be accomplished effort, it is, in a very real sense, fortunate that the context for solution of foreseeable problems of dislocation will be far wider than the problems themselves. This is because the less developed nations around the world can provide a virtually limitless market for the products of American technological innovation, not only in terms of goods, but of people as well. Probing the depth of that market, and of the mechanisms of capital and investment that will be required to generate and sustain significant transfer, is beyond the scope of this report. Nonetheless, this study will fill a vitally useful function by underlining the availability of American scientific and technical resources in the event of significant arms reductions. It can suggest to scholars, governments and international organizations the urgency of mounting similar studies of the opportunities in specific developing countries which industries as well as individuals freed from defense work

— not only American but from other developed countries as well — could serve.

One immediate and tangible step to facilitate an international solution of the redeployment problems of nations undertaking arms reductions could be taken which need not await further progress in the interminable negotiations toward arms control: A register of specific employment opportunities for scientists and engineers could be created by the United Nations or one of its specialized agencies, listing schools, universities and research facilities in developing countries to which personnel in countries most affected by disarmament could turn for placement in areas where their skills are urgently needed. Once such a register is in being, capital to sponsor the transfer of individual scientists and engineers might become readily available, from both public and private quarters, to support the scientific "Peace Corps" that might ultimately emerge. The willingness of qualified researchers and teachers to serve might generate the founding of wholly new institutions or the expansion of existing ones and the provision of new scientific equipment hitherto unavailable for want of confidence in the ability of developing countries to supply necessary skilled personnel.

Establishing such a service need not wait for the onset of disarmament, however, for present needs are great, and the willingness of scientists and engineers to commit themselves to the problems of developing countries may even exceed the assumptions on which this proposal is based. Of all the conceivable methods of international cooperation, the early availability of such a mechanism to help transfer the skills and energies of scientific and technical workers from swords to ploughshares would be a most practical and symbolic step.

REFERENCES

1. U. S. Congress, Joint Economic Committee, *Economic Indicators*, July 1966 (Washington, D. C., U.S.G. P.O.), pp. 1 and 11.

2. Lecht, Leonard A., *Goals, Priorities, and Dollars*, A Study of the National Planning Association Center for Priority Analysis, The Free Press, New York, 1966, p. 21.

3. One serious student of the economic aspects of disarmament, Professor Emile Benoit of Columbia University, has prepared estimates of additional national expenditures required during the 1960's for various domestic and international goals, totalling between 65.0 and 67.4 billion dollars more than the nation's entire annual expenditure on defense. Professor Benoit's projections, moreover, omit space as an additional claimant on America's resources. Emile Benoit, "Alternatives to Defense Production," in Benoit and Boulding, *Disarmament and the Economy*, Harper & Row, New York, 1963, pp. 218-19

4. See President Lyndon B. Johnson's defense message to Congress, January 18, 1965, presented in the *Department of State Bulletin*, February 15, 1965, pp. 211-18 in which the President forecast in guarded, but hopeful, terms an essentially steady defense budget:

Barring a significant shift in the international situation, we are not likely to require further increments on so large a scale during the next several years. Expenditures for defense will thus constitute a declining portion of our expanding annual gross national product, which is now growing at the rate of 5 percent each year. If, over the next several years, we continue to spend approximately the same amount of dollars annually for our national defense that we are spending today, an even larger share of our expanding wealth will be free to meet our vital needs, both public and private . . .", p. 217.

For the purposes of formulating this parameter, it is assumed that international conditions would not justify the procurement of a major anti-ballistic missile (ABM) defense system for the continental United States.

5. Gilpatric, Roswell L., "Our Defense Needs: The Long View," in *Foreign Affairs,* April 1964, pp. 366-78.

6. See United Nations Disarmament Commission, "Memorandum of the United States on Measures to Stop the Spread of Nuclear Weapons, Halt and Turn Down the Arms Race, and Reduce International Tension," DC/214/Add. 1, April 29, 1965, pp. 9-11.

7. See U. S. "Outline of Basic Provisions of a Treaty on General and Complete Disarmament in a Peaceful World," April 18, 1962.

8. A notable exception to the general rule is a study by the National Planning Association on "Community Adjustment of Reduced Defense Spending," completed for the U. S. Arms Control and Disarmament Agency in December 1965, in which the impact of these alternative arms reductions was closely examined for three specific defense-impacted communities. See U. S. Arms Control and Disarmament Agency, *Community Adjustment to Reduced Defense Spending: Case Studies of Potential Impact on Seattle-Tacoma, Baltimore and New London-Groton-Nor-*

wich, Report prepared for the National Planning Association, Center for Economic Projections (Washington, U.S.G.P.O., 1965).

9. An important basic tool for forecasting the sales and job consequences of specific reductions and shifts from defense expenditures has been developed by Wassily Leontief and Marvin Hoffenberg in their article, "The Economic Effects of Disarmament," *Scientific American,* April 1961, pp. 47-55, in which Leontief's input-output method of analysis is applied to a 1958 national model of industry relationships.

10. *Report of the Committee on the Economic Impact of Defense and Disarmament,* July 1965 (Washington, U.S.G.P.O., 1965), p. 6.

11. Cited in *Manpower Report of the President,* 1965, p. 66.

12. Nelson, Richard R., "The Impact of Disarmament on Research and Development." This study has appeared in several publications and is here cited from Benoit and Boulding, *op. cit.,* pp. 112-28.

13. *Ibid.,* p. 119.

14. *Ibid.,* p. 125.

15. *Report of the Committee on the Economic Impact of Defense and Disarmament, op. cit.,* p. 19.

16. Weidenbaum, Murray L., "Problems of Adjustment," in Benoit and Boulding, *op. cit.,* p. 84.

17. Arthur D. Little, Inc., "Strategies for Survival in the Aero-space Industry" by Thomas G. Miller, Jr., Cambridge, Mass., 1964, p. 26.

18. *Ibid.,* p. 26.

19. See Michaelis, Michael, "Opportunities and Problems in Technical Innovation: the 'Systems' Approach," in *Convertibility of Space and Defense Re-*

sources to Civilian Needs: A Search for New Employ-ment Potentials, compiled for the subcommittee on Employment and Manpower of the Committee on Labor and Public Welfare, U. S. Senate (Washington, U.S.G.P.O., 1964), pp. 872—5.

20. See Bainbridge, John, "Reporter at Large: Camp Kilmer" in *The New Yorker,* May 21, 1966, p. 112.

21. *Aerospace Facts and Figures,* 1960 edition, Aerospace Industries Association, p. 86, quoted in Benoit and Boulding, *op. cit.,* p. 81.

22. U. S. Arms Control and Disarmament Agency, *Defense Industry Diversification,* A Report prepared by John S. Gilmore and Dean Coddington, University of Denver Research Institute (Washington, U.S.G.P.O., 1966).

23. U. S. Arms Control and Disarmament Agency, *Industrial Conversion Potential in the Shipbuilding Industry,* A Report prepared by William R. Park and Robert E. Roberts, Midwest Research Institute (Washington, U.S.G.P.O., 1966).

24. U. S. Arms Control and Disarmament Agency, *Implications of Reduced Defense Demand for the Electronics Industry.* A Report prepared by Battelle Memorial Institute (Washington, U.S.G.P.O., 1965).

25. *Ibid.,* p. 51.

26. Quotations from *Ibid.,* pp. 60-61.

27. Colm, Gerhard and Lecht, Leonard A., "Requirements of Scientific and Engineering Manpower in the 1970's," in *Toward Better Utilization of Scientific and Engineering Talent, A Program for Action,* National Academy of Sciences, Washington, 1964, p. 75.

28. See, for example, The President's Science Advisory Committee, *Meeting Manpower Needs in Science and Technology, Report Number One: Graduate Train-*

ing in Engineering, Mathematics, and Physical Sciences, The White House (Washington, U.S.G.P.O., 1962).

29. See *Journal of Engineering Education,* Vol. 56, December 1965, p. 108.

30. Manpower Report of the President, 1965, p. 67.

31. U. S. Arms Control and Disarmament Agency, *The Dyna-Soar Contract Cancellation,* A Report by the State of Washington, Employment Security Department (Washington, U.S.G.P.O., 1965).

32. U. S. Arms Control and Disarmament Agency, *Community Adjustment to Reduced Defense Spending, etc., op. cit.*

33. Solow, R., "Technical Change and Aggregate Production Function," *The Review of Economics and Statistics,* Vol. 39 (August 1957), pp. 312—20.

34. National Commission on Technology, Automation, and Economic Progress, *Technology and the American Economy* (Washington, U.S.G.P.O., February 1966), Vol. II, p. 87.

35. *Ibid.,* p. 84.

36. National Science Foundation, *Research and Development in Industry,* , pp. 49, 64, 81, and *Research and Developement in Industry,* , pp. 12, 40; quoted in *Goals, Priorities, and Dollars, op. cit.,* pp. 174—5.

37. *The New York Times,* August 5, 1965.

38. Federal Council for Science and Technology. *Report to the President on Water Resources Research.* A report of its Coordinated Task Group on Water Resources Research. Published as a Committee Print of the Senate Committee on Interior and Insular Affairs, 88th Congress, 1st session, February 11, 1963 (Washington: U.S.G.P.O.).

39. National Academy of Sciences, Panel on Weather and Climate Modification, *Weather and Climate Modifications, Problems and Prospects,* Vol. I (Washington, 1966), p. 2.

40. Armer, Paul, "Computer Applications of Technological Change, Automation and Economic Progress," The Rand Corporation (mimeo), study prepared for The National Commission on Technology, Automation and Economic Progress, p. 7.

41. Seidman, Philip, "In Electronics the Big Stakes Ride on Tiny Chips," *Fortune,* June 1966, pp. 120ff.

42. "Innovation and Experimentation in Education," Report of a Panel of the President's Science Advisory Committee, The White House (Washington, U.S.G.P. O., 1964), p. 1.

43. *Report of the Committee on the Economic Impact of Defense and Disarmament, op. cit.,* p. 28.

44. U.S. Congress, House Committee on Government Operations, 89th Congress, 2nd Session: *The Federal Research and Development Programs: The Decision-making Process;* Washington, U.S.G.P.O., June 27, 1966.